Canadian-American Trade and Investment under the Free Trade Agreement

CANADIAN-AMERICAN TRADE AND INVESTMENT UNDER THE FREE TRADE AGREEMENT

Harold Crookell
Foreword by DAVID S. R. LEIGHTON

Q

QUORUM BOOKS
NEW YORK • WESTPORT, CONNECTICUT • LONDON

Library of Congress Cataloging-in-Publication Data

Crookell, H. (Harold).
        Canadian-American trade and investment under the Free Trade
Agreement / Harold Crookell.
        p.   cm.
        ISBN 0–89930–481–8 (alk. paper)
        1. Free trade—United States.   2. Free trade—Canada.   3. Tariff—
United States.   4. Tariff—Canada.   5. United States—Commerce—
Canada.   6. Canada—Commerce—United States.   7. Canada.   Treaties,
etc.   United States, 1988 Jan. 2.   8. Competition, International.
I. Title.
HF1456.C765   1990
382′.0971073—dc20   90–32922

British Library Cataloguing in Publication Data is available.

Library of Congress Catalog Card Number: 90–32922
ISBN: 0–89930–481–8

First published in 1990

Quorum Books, 88 Post Road West, Westport, CT 06881
An imprint of Greenwood Publishing Group, Inc.

Printed in the United States of America

The paper used in this book complies with the
Permanent Paper Standard issued by the National
Information Standards Organization (Z39.48–1984).

10 9 8 7 6 5 4 3 2 1

Copyright Acknowledgments

The following sources have granted permission to reprint material:

Material reprinted from the Department of External Affairs, Canada, *The Canada-U.S. Free Trade Agreement: Synopsis*, second edition (1988) is reproduced with permission of the Minister of Supply and Services Canada, 1989.

"Maclean's/Decima Poll," from *Maclean's*, July 3, 1989, is reprinted courtesy of *Maclean's*, Toronto, Canada.

To my father, who taught me to respect people
of all nationalities

CONTENTS

ILLUSTRATIONS

Figures

Tables

FOREWORD

When Harold Crookell asked me if I would write a foreword for this book, I had no hesitation in agreeing, for both professional and personal reasons. This is an important book. It deals with a vital area of interest to both American and Canadian businessmen. And it represents the distillation of the views and experience of one of our most highly-qualified commentators.

Professor Crookell has been observing, teaching and writing on the subject of U.S.–Canada business for over 20 years. That alone would command our attention. But he has not been just a distant, arms-length observer. He has been intimately involved, on both sides of the border, with corporations as they struggle with the realities of corporate strategy and its implementation.

No dry, academic tome this. The author's wry sense of humor and vivid metaphors enliven a subject that is of the utmost seriousness and importance to top managers in both Canadian and U.S. business. The analysis, diagnosis and prescriptions address what we instinctively know are real-world, urgent issues. The words ring true. The result is a volume that promises to contribute much to the resolution of problems faced by policymakers and managers in both government and business. It is a good example of how our academic community can contribute to the solution of society's problems.

To facilitate this process is precisely the mission of the National Centre for Management Research and Development. But in addition to this professional fit, there is a personal dimension as well. Harold Crookell has been a friend and colleague for many years, one whose accomplishments have been a great source of both pleasure and admiration.

David S. R. Leighton
Director
National Centre for Management Research
and Development
London, Ontario

PREFACE

Trying to write a book in 1990 is a challenging experience. So much is changing in the world so quickly and so decisively that nothing stays constant long enough to capture events and it is virtually impossible to predict the future. One of the constants standing out in the turmoil is the decline of national sovereignty and the globalization of world markets. The U.S.-Canada Free Trade Agreement, Europe 1992, the transformation of Eastern Europe, and the rise of Japan and the four tigers can all be seen either as steps toward globalization or as by-products of it.

This book focuses on a major North American response to globalization: the U.S.-Canada Free Trade Agreement, and how it is likely to affect parents and subsidiaries in the U.S. and Canada. A free trade agreement between nations is rather like a marriage: it attempts to bind the two parties closer together. But it is not as traditional a marriage as Europe is entering into with its much more binding 1992 initiative. The U.S.-Canada Agreement seeks mutual economic benefit without the surrender of political independence. It is a modern marriage, if you will. Each partner retains a distinct identity. No attempt is made to force change on either partner. Desirable change is expected to arise from the closer affiliation of the two nations. The free trade dream is one of voluntary cooperation for economic benefit between increasingly interdependent nations. To make it work the two nations have to understand one another better over time, and the success of the relationship has to matter to both.

When the U.S.-Canada Free Trade Agreement became effective on January 1, 1989, reactions in the two countries signalled the likelihood of troubled times ahead. When one spouse is distracted on the wedding night, one might reasonably question the future of the marriage. The United States was the distracted spouse. It was marrying Canada—its largest trading partner, but its attention was on Japan—its second largest trading partner. Canada had a massive national debate over the Free Trade Agreement. It contained a unique blend of national patriotism, anti-American sentiment, and a dawning realization of the difficult challenge globalization presented to Canada. In the final analysis, Canadians voted for free trade. The twin contemporary pressures of globalization and the knowledge-based economy won out over the pull of history and tradition. Canada entered the marriage with its national mind made up. The United States did not.

I visited San Diego in November 1988 to attend an international business conference. Canada's traumatic free trade election was just finished, and the U.S. presidential election was in its final stages. My visit left a deep impression on me. I had been very involved in the free trade debate in Canada. It had consumed a lot of my time and thought. As I listened to the Bush-Dukakis presidential debate, it became clear that the Free Trade Agreement with Canada was not a hot political topic in the United States. It wasn't even a cold topic. It simply didn't matter. To make things worse, it wasn't even on the conference agenda. Europe 1992 was on the agenda; it was still four years off and most of the speakers politely concluded that it was unlikely to materialize anyway. The Canada-U.S. Agreement was set to go into effect within two months and it just didn't warrant attention. Something inside me stirred and the seed for this book took root. What sustained it through months of difficult writing, however, was something else entirely—something that is not easy to express on paper.

I liked San Diego. The warmth of its people, its impressive parks, and old Spanish architecture, the quaintness of Old Town and the imaginative development of its harbor. I would have liked to stay longer. I felt at home there as I have in many other American cities. It began to dawn on me that I really wanted this free trade marriage to succeed, and that improved understanding of one another's hopes and aspirations was an important prerequisite. Of course, there are many fascinating places and cultures in other parts of the world too, but the United States comes in for so much of the world's criticism and condescension that for an outsider to praise it for its openness, warmth and vitality is perhaps long overdue. In any event, I for one would like to see this marriage between two great nations succeed, anchored in a foundation of genuine understanding and interdependence. My hope is that this book will pour some much needed cement on that foundation.

The first chapter touches briefly on the history of Canada-U.S. dialogue on free trade over the past 130 years. It is interesting that in 1854, before Canada was a nation, Great Britain and the United States signed a North American Trade Agreement, which was abrogated by the United States in 1866 because of internal pressures. It has taken over 120 years of intermittent trying and a dramatic change in the competitive environment to put it back in place. Chapter 2 touches on some of the important aspects of the Free Trade Agreement and contrasts them with the key thrust of the Europe 1992 initiative which is altogether different. A detailed summary of the Agreement prepared by the Canadian government appears as an appendix to the book for those readers interested in specific details. In another appendix, a 1989 Maclean's survey of Canadian and American attitudes on various issues is reproduced to underline where similarities and differences are most pronounced.

The third chapter deals with the different challenges facing our two countries in overcoming the legacy of protectionism. Canada's challenges include the dismantling of internal trade barriers between provinces, the reharnessing of trade union power and reshaping of the economic role of government. America's challenge is the rejection of Fortress North America and hence a calmer look at the dangers of managed trade, voluntary export restraints, level playing fields and trade reciprocity.

Chapters 4 and 5 deal with issues of globalization and parent-subsidiary relations respectively. Globalization is responsible for distracting the United States on the eve of its free trade marriage to Canada. It is a legitimate distraction. American business has to come to grips with the great global triad—Europe, Japan and North America. The challenge is reshaping how American firms compete in world markets, which in turn is changing the relationships between American parents and their subsidiaries. How American subsidiaries in Canada respond to the challenge of free trade is enormously important to Canada—about forty percent of Canada's manufacturing output is in their hands. What role can they play in the competitive global strategies of their parents? This is a complex and vital question not only for Canada, but also for the United States which faces large inflows of foreign direct investment itself. Globalization is expected to lead us toward greater interdependence between nations. This creative middle ground between independence and dependence reflects a growing concern over global inequities and global preservation. The challenge for international firms is to put a healthy measure of interdependence into their global organizations and to transform their subsidiaries into competitive affiliates. How this is carried out in practice is a particularly sensitive concern in Canada.

The final chapter is somewhat futuristic; not in the crystal ball tradition, but in terms of clear evidence of where we are headed. The Free Trade Agreement has been signed and is in effect, but there are many unresolved issues still being negotiated including the elusive question of what constitutes a subsidy for unfair trade purposes. A lot of goodwill is going to be needed between Canada and the United States to resolve these issues in the decade ahead. At the same time both nations have to make adjustments to improve the competitiveness and educational standards of their societies. For Canada, the gut-wrenching election debate over the Free Trade Agreement has paved the way for change. For the United States, it is Japan's success that generates the greatest pressure for change. Nothing written in Canada is ever likely to galvanize American reaction the way Ishihara and Morita's "The Japan That Can Say 'No' " (1989) has. It may well be the first best seller never to be published. The hope of this book is more modest. The Canada-U.S. relationship needs to be on the agenda during the next decade or the marriage will never make it and that would be a shame. Growing together interdependently takes mutual understanding and a desire to succeed. This book is a small step down that road.

On a personal level, the real impetus to write the book came from three sources. First was the major free trade debate in Canada which forced me to think through my own views more thoroughly and to make them public. Second was the encouragement of my wife, Doreen, who saw that my twenty plus years of academic work in international business and business-government relations had prepared me in a unique way to say something about globalization and the Free Trade Agreement. And, third was the perseverance of Tom Gannon at Quorum Books who kept the project alive by his frequent phone calls when I felt least like writing. Once the project was underway, David Leighton, director of Canada's National Centre for Management Research and Development had a positive influence which resulted in our joint development of a management seminar to help business executives manage the transition to free trade and globalization. The National Centre also assisted with some of the preproduction costs of the book.

While many of the ideas expressed in this book owe their origin to other authors, to academic colleagues and to business executives in both Canada and the United States, I accept full responsibility for how they are expressed in this book. My wife pored over earlier drafts and made a number of very helpful suggestions to broaden the appeal of the book. My thanks go to her in many ways. She knows a lot about how to make an interdependent relationship work.

Typing of the manuscript was handled by Phyllis Jackson, whose patient professionalism and cheerful disposition made the task more pleasant. We both thank modern technology for making it easier to erase the past.

Canadian-American Trade and
Investment under the Free
Trade Agreement

1

AN ERA OF FREE TRADE

The United States and Canada launched a comprehensive free trade agreement on January 1, 1989, yet six months later almost half of Americans surveyed were not even aware of it. Since the agreement is an important step toward the kind of national interdependence required by the increasing globalization of markets, it warrants attention. Furthermore, the implementation phase is not likely to be smooth unless there is a clear understanding of each nation's goals and concerns in entering the agreement. That understanding is deficient at present in both countries, but especially in the United States.

In the fall of 1988 both Canada and the United States held general elections, and both returned "conservative" leaders through democratic processes. But there were few other similarities between the two elections. In terms of substantive content, there was no similarity at all. Canadians held a fierce emotion-laden debate about the Canada-U.S. Free Trade Agreement. It was at times passionate, patriotic, bitter and divisive, but seldom informative. Nevertheless it was held. "Free trade" was not just the main theme of the Canadian election, it was the only theme. Every office, every club, every home, every social occasion was the site of a minidebate. Newspapers, journals, letters to editors and television and radio broadcasts focussed on "free trade." It was no great surprise, therefore, to discover in a national poll (see appendix A) reported in *Maclean's* on July 3, 1989, that only 3 percent of Canadians were unaware that Canada and the United States had signed a free trade agreement.

When the same question was put to a sample of 1,000 Americans, 43 percent indicated that they were unaware of the agreement—a huge difference, but not a surprising one given the general lack of free trade discussion in the United States. Tribute is owed to the 57 percent who were aware of the agreement, in view of the absence of U.S. media coverage. The Canada-U.S. Free Trade Agreement was not even a minor theme in the U.S. elections. There was no passion, no divisiveness and no bitterness over it—just a giant national yawn. Of course, many Americans yawned over the entire 1988 election process: campaigns consisted largely of paid advertisements, and debates consisted of sequential prepared speeches. Nevertheless, it was significant that the hottest issue in the Canadian election never really came to the surface in the United States. It was as though the two nations were on different planets rather than being next-door neighbours.

There are several compelling reasons why the free trade debate was so much more intense in Canada than in the United States, but still the absence of debate in the United States is worrying. The newly signed agreement is comprehensive in its scope. It is a bold initiative embracing trade in services as well as goods. Mechanisms have been established to resolve trade disputes. Political integration is not part of the agreement: it is not like the European Economic Community (EEC) initiative. It is aimed primarily at increased economic cooperation. Many Canadians are afraid that increased economic cooperation will lead inexorably to increased political integration and subsequent loss of Canadian sovereignty and identity. The agreement is written as though this fear is unfounded. It attempts to ensure economic gains without corresponding political "losses"; to move from independence to interdependence in economic affairs. The journey will be fraught with dangers and, if not managed well, could lead us where neither nation really wants to go. Both nations can gain from working together more closely in economic affairs. But if over time working together develops into a dependent rather than an interdependent relationship, the resulting divorce will be very costly indeed. Canada and the United States have embarked on a kind of mutually beneficial economic marriage. Whether it succeeds will depend on how well the two nations understand and respond to one another's needs, and on how much space they allow each other to express their own individuality. Because Canada is by far the smaller partner in economic terms, it has been the more concerned about the details of the agreement in advance. But now that the agreement is signed, the United States must become more concerned too.

That is why this book is being written. There has been little substantive debate in the United States about entering the Free Trade Agreement with Canada. The understanding needed to make a success of the emerging new relationship may not be deep enough. Since the agreement is essentially an economic one, it is in the business community that increased understanding may be most needed. This book tries to explain important aspects of the Canada-U.S. Free Trade Agreement in nontechnical language for American business managers, who over the next few years will make decisions of far-reaching consequence for Canadians. It is written in part to explain Canadian concerns to Americans, and in part to explore possible avenues of action that may not be considered without an understanding of those concerns. The perspective of the author is essentially pragmatic. Within the context of a basically competitive environment, the desire is to improve the long-run chances of success for the economic marriage the United States and Canada have embarked upon.

A HISTORICAL PERSPECTIVE

The Canada-U.S. Free Trade Agreement took effect on January 1, 1989. It was concluded and initialled on October 4, 1987, and approved relatively quietly by the U.S. Senate on September 19, 1988, and relatively noisily in Canada's House of Commons in December 1988. It was a triumph that 130 years of previous efforts had failed to achieve. Free trade has been on the Canada-U.S. agenda on several previous occasions dating as far back as 1854, when an agreement of sorts was actually signed, only to be terminated in 1866 by the United States. The next 45 years were characterized by repeated efforts first by Canada and then by the United States to reestablish a trade pact, but protectionism first in the United States, then in Canada, blocked progress. A flurry of activity in 1911 brought about an "informal" trade agreement documented largely by an exchange of letters, but Canada's Liberal party that negotiated it lost an election over it, and it was never implemented. After 1911 protectionism took hold in both countries, and no further bilateral negotiations were held until 1935, when a modest most-favored-nation agreement was negotiated, and again in 1948. Little is known about the 1948 negotiations except that they were broken off by the Canadian government. One likely reason is that Canadian politicians thought that they could do better as a small nation negotiating through the General Agreement on Tariffs and Trade (GATT), which was signed in October 1947, than bilaterally with the United States. Why these earlier negotiations failed and the latest ones succeeded is an interesting question. It is useful to address it through a closer examination of the historic negotiations and a comparison to the current economic environment.

The 1854 Agreement

The reciprocal free trade agreement of 1854 was actually negotiated between the United States and Great Britain. Canada at the time consisted of five colonial provinces: Canada (now Ontario and Quebec), New Brunswick, Nova Scotia, Prince Edward Island and Newfoundland. The provinces had not yet achieved nationhood; in fact, it was only in 1850 that they formed a free trade association between themselves. So Britain negotiated on their behalf, and Britain, having adopted a policy of universal free trade in 1846, was positively disposed from the outset. There were, however, two more immediate issues that put pressure on the negotiations: one was an economic depression in the late 1840s that Britain feared might encourage the provinces to move toward union with the United States, and the other was a dispute over North Atlantic fishing rights that the treaty helped to resolve.

The commodities covered by the agreement were essentially natural resources and agricultural products (including fish, grain, flour, animals, dairy products, timber, coal, dried fruits, firewood and unmanufactured tobacco). Manufactured goods were not in general included in the agreement, partly because of fear of Britain's strength in manufacturing and partly because of the dependence of the provinces on customs revenue from imports of manufactures. Nevertheless, it appears that almost two-thirds of the total merchandise trade between the thirty states then in the American union and the five "Canadian" provinces became duty free under the agreement. At the same time trade patterns were not much altered by the agreement, just facilitated. Most of the articles included in the agreement were already widely traded, so tariff removal merely made trade more convenient.

Since the 1854 treaty was a free trade agreement rather than a customs union (or common market), both sides remained free to set their own tariffs on goods from third countries. Britain encouraged its five colonies to extend the terms of the treaty to all other trading nations, but the provinces—other than Prince Edward Island—dragged their heels, and the United States was not anxious to extend the treaty either. As a result, it remained essentially a North American agreement. During the life of the treaty, a number of attempts—mostly but not entirely from the United States—were made to transform it into a full customs union. A quote from the American poet Walt Whitman captures the mood of the time and suggests that the major stumbling block to a customs union was Canada's attachment to England.

Some of the more liberal of the presses here are discussing the question of a *zollverein* between the United States and

Canada. It is proposed to form a union for commercial purposes—to altogether abolish the frontier tariff line, with its double sets of customhouse officials now existing between the two countries, and to agree upon one tariff for both, the proceeds of this tariff to be divided between the two governments on the basis of population. It is said that a large proportion of the merchants of Canada are in favor of this step, as they believe it would materially add to the business of the country, by removing the restrictions that now exist on trade between Canada and the States. Those persons who are opposed to the measure believe that it would increase the material welfare of the country, but it would loosen the bonds between Canada and England; and this sentiment overrides the desire for commercial prosperity. Whether the sentiment can continue to bear the strain put upon it is a question. It is thought by many that commercial considerations must in the end prevail. It seems also to be generally agreed that such a *zollverein*, or common customs union, would bring practically more benefits to the Canadian provinces than to the United States.[1]

Attempts to turn the treaty into a customs union were brought to a sudden end in 1866 when the United States terminated the reciprocal free trade agreement despite its relative popularity. The main reasons for the American action appeared to stem from political problems related to the American Civil War. There was also a minor dispute because Canada increased its tariffs on manufactured goods in 1859 to raise government revenues, and the United States objected. However, since very few manufactured goods were included in the agreement, this could not have been such a major issue. More to the point was the protectionism that developed in the United States during and after the Civil War. Canadians made repeated attempts to reestablish the treaty over the next twenty years and extended a standing offer of reciprocity that was never taken up. When American protectionism began to recede in the late 1880s, Canada had already embarked on its own protectionist National Policy and was not in the mood for U.S. overtures. Furthermore, U.S. overtures in the 1890s took the form of proposals for a full customs union, and Canada was not willing to include manufactured goods or risk loosening its ties to the Commonwealth, which was then its largest trading partner.

The 1911 Agreement

The impetus to try for another agreement arose from a tariff war that broke out in 1907. Canada's membership in the Commonwealth was at the root of it. In 1907 Canada adopted a three-tiered tariff system with Commonwealth nations at the top and the United States conspicuously at the bottom. The American Tariff Act of 1909 represented the retaliation, and the war was on. Canadian delegates went to Washington in January 1911 to try to defuse things and came away with a rapidly concluded oral agreement by January 16. No treaty was signed, but the Canadian delegates put their understanding of the agreement into a formal letter, and U.S. Secretary of State Philander Knox made a formal reply. By this time, the Dominion of Canada had been formed, so Canadians did their own negotiating on behalf of the Dominion as a whole. This proved to be the undoing of the 1911 agreement. When Britain did the negotiating, the Canadian provinces had merely to ratify the result, and confidence in Britain's negotiating skill and strength was fairly high. When the Canadian government did its own negotiating and then had to face a general election on the results, the confidence of Canadians was not forthcoming, and the election was lost. The 1911 agreement was never implemented.

What the 1911 agreement attempted was somewhat more modest than the 1854 treaty but involved a wider array of products. The 1911 agreement was seen as a step toward a treaty. It involved tariff elimination on some products (Schedule A, natural resources, the easy ones to deal with), and tariff reductions on other products (Schedule B, manufactured goods made from the natural resources). In addition, Canada agreed to reduce duties on imports of coal, cement, fruit trees and some foodstuffs from the United States, and the United States agreed to reduce duties on imports of planed wood, shingles, iron ore and aluminum from Canada. The hope on both sides appeared to be that the agreement might grow into a treaty over time by shifting more and more goods into the Schedule A category. Evidently, a more modest beginning was thought to improve the likelihood of getting the initiative accepted by both legislatures. While the U.S. Congress did accept it in 1911, the Liberal government in Canada that had sponsored it went down to electoral defeat at the hands of the Conservatives, who campaigned vigorously against it. There was almost a repeat in 1988. Congress approved the current agreement, but Canada came close to rejecting it in an election. This time, however, it was the Conservative party that sponsored the agreement and the Liberal party that campaigned vigorously against it. Such are the vagaries of politics.

WHY DID THE 1988 AGREEMENT SUCCEED?

While much of the rhetoric in Canada's election campaign had shades of prior decades, economic circumstances had changed a lot. From Canada's perspective, the United States was now by far its largest trading partner, and ties to Britain were loosened when Britain chose to enter the EEC. Furthermore, tariffs were no longer such a major contributor to government revenues. From the U.S. perspective, Canada was now its largest trading partner, although many Americans thought that it was Japan, and the United States was continuing to urge all nations to liberalize trade through the GATT. The United States faced a particularly difficult problem in 1987–88 in the size of its trade deficit. It was losing market share in world trade in manufactures to Japan, Germany and the Far East. In its areas of strength—technology and services—it was facing a variety of nontariff impediments in major markets of the world. The U.S. interest was to open world markets in its areas of strength as well as to improve its performance in world trade. While there was much protectionist fervor in the United States, Americans, in general, were not persuaded that protectionism was the way to go. Protectionism was not a winning theme in the 1988 presidential election. The ground was therefore suitably prepared for another Canada-U.S. free trade initiative.

Two other important factors were also at play that undoubtedly improved the climate for a new initiative: one was the decline in national sovereignty and the other the rise in globalization of business activity. The two factors are intertwined, but it is worth examining them separately.

The Decline of Sovereignty

The importance of national sovereignty declined in the 1980s because the prices of natural resources declined. Throughout the 1970s resource prices rose, increasing the wealth of resource-rich countries like Canada and increasing their interest in sovereignty. Sovereignty was seen as important because it was the basis for ownership of the resources. Two-hundred–mile "fishing limits" became a way to lay claim to underwater deposits of oil or other minerals. The world appeared to be short of resources, so Canada's future wealth seemed secure because of escalating prices. Government was important as titular owner of national resources and as distributor of the wealth among the people. In this scenario sovereignty mattered. The 1981–82 recession came as a cruel shock in Canada and damaged Canadians' confidence in their government. The subsequent economic recovery, which, in Canada, was precipitated by a recovery in the United States, left Canadians puzzled by the fact that natural-resource prices did not recover with it. Subsequent analysis showed that the "recovery" was actually more like a transformation. New industries grew more than old ones, and old industries learned to function with fewer natural resources. The idea of global resource shortages failed to take hold. Instead we talked of the knowledge revolution, reflecting the rapid growth of knowledge-based industries. Canada was not at a competitive disadvantage in the knowledge revolution: it had considerable strength in communications technology, engineering, education, software and other fields. But sovereignty and nationalism did not fit the emerging economy the way they did the resource-rich era of the seventies. The knowledge era required nations to be in the flow of ideas or be left behind. It required interdependence just as much as the resource era required independence. The transition from a resource-based to a knowledge-based era therefore required a transition in political thinking from independence to interdependence. In such a transition sovereignty and nationalism are natural casualties, and sovereignty and nationalism tend for many to go hand in hand with protectionism—nasty bedfellows though they are.

The Rise of Globalization

The globalization of business activity has been made possible, of course, by the gradual demise of tariffs, protectionism and national sovereignty. It has also been made possible by technology—on the supply side by computer communication and fax machines that make it easier to run a global business, and on the demand side by satellite television and growing world travel that make global consumer tastes more similar. But the massive contributor to globalization has been the way Japanese businesses have won market share through global strategies and global branding of products designed from the outset for world markets. Others are following suit. International acquisitions are on the rise. Nation-state power is in retreat. The success of Japan has demonstrated for others that the market economy really is free in that the powerful and entrenched nations can be outperformed in competition. Europe 1992 can be seen as an attempt to increase the efficiency of the EEC to counter the threat from Japan. *Perestroika* and the emergence of Eastern Europe can be seen as a rejection of isolationism, both because technology has made it impractical and because opportunity has made it unwise. The Canada-U.S. Free Trade Agreement can be seen as North America's move to increase efficiency to counter the Japanese challenge. Globalization is changing the economic landscape with startling rapidity. Canada cannot afford to be left behind. Mexico may wish to participate in time also. The opportunity should not be closed. Growth within major trading blocs will enhance their efficiency, and openness between blocs will enhance their effectiveness over time.

WHY ARE CANADIANS STILL WORRIED?

In view of the developments in the global economy that point so clearly to the need for closer interdependence between Canada and the United States, why are Canadians still worried about the Free Trade Agreement? Why was it almost rejected in Canada's 1988 election, whereas it passed with relative ease in the United States? Are Canadians still steeped in the past, or do they have some genuine concerns that Americans do not have? If so, what are they?

The joke is told in Canada about the chicken and the pig chatting in the farmyard when a truck rolled by bearing the label, "Eat ham and eggs for breakfast." "What do you think of that?" said the chicken. "It's alright for you," replied the pig. "You just make a contribution, but for me it's a total commitment." In the Free Trade Agreement Canada is somewhat like the pig. Because Canada's economy is so much smaller than that of the United States, it faces the high-risk–high-return end of the agreement while the United States faces the low-risk–low-return end. It is useful to understand why this is so. The United States under the Free Trade Agreement obtains tariff-free access to a market one-tenth the size of its own. American businesses will not have to invest heavily to seize the opportunities thus opened. The adjustment is one that can be taken in stride. For Canada, of course, the opposite is true. The Free Trade Agreement will require a major adjustment for Canadian businesses because they are faced with improved access to a market ten times the size of their own. To seize the enormous opportunities presented, Canadian firms have to specialize their product lines and export to the United States. Heavy investment will be required to restructure Canadian industry, and Canadian productivity will have to improve. The adjustment challenge will be a tough one, but extraordinary progress usually has a price.

One result of all this is that Canadians feel more vulnerable than Americans to the possibility of the agreement being terminated.

From a business point of view, if an American firm manages to secure the same market share for its products in Canada as it has in the United States, it will end up exporting about 10 percent of its output. If, on the other hand, a Canadian firm secures the same market share in the United States as it has in Canada, it will end up exporting over 90 percent of its output. It is not difficult to see which firm is more vulnerable in the event that the agreement is abrogated. The American firm would be inconvenienced, while the Canadian firm would be shattered. In spite of the vulnerability, Canadian firms have to pursue the American market because they cannot get their costs down to competitive levels unless they do. For Canada it is a total commitment.

This sensitivity to size is well developed in Canada. David-and-Goliath images are common. More common for some reason is the image of the elephant and the mouse. The Canadian trade negotiator's office in Ottawa sported an elephant-and-mouse painting on the wall during the Free Trade Agreement negotiations. When the elephant sneezes, the mouse catches flu. Marriage to an elephant increases the vulnerability. It may roll over in bed and, however well intentioned, may terminate the mouse. The European Common Market worked because the participating countries were of similar size and different languages. For Canada and the United States the reverse is true. Canadians feel a risk of being swamped economically, culturally and politically by the "friendly giant" to the south. It is not that Canadians suspect American motives in signing the agreement; it is more a sense that Americans do not know much about Canadians and could easily do something harmful quite inadvertently. The 1989 *Maclean's* poll tended to confirm this concern (see Apendix A). Only 11 percent of Americans even knew the name of Canada's prime minister, and 66 percent of Americans would like to see Canada become the fifty-first state of the United States, while 85 percent of Canadians would not. Ask Americans who their largest trading partner is, and 69 percent say it is Japan. The correct answer is Canada: Canada-U.S. two-way trade was around Canadian $186.4 billion in 1988. Canadians feel irritated and overlooked. When the current Canada-U.S. Free

Trade Agreement was initialled in October 1987, media coverage in Canada was very extensive. In the United States it was a nonevent. I asked an American colleague why this was, and he responded with a story about an American and a Japanese business executive sentenced to death in the Middle East and offered one last request. The Japanese executive said, "I'd just like to take a few minutes to explain why Japan has been so successful in world markets over the past decade." The American promptly responded, "I'd just like to die before I have to listen to one more lecture about the superiority of Japanese management." My colleague went on to explain that the United States was preoccupied with Japan. The United States was under attack commercially and had to focus its energy. Canadians, however, are concerned that U.S. understanding of Canada was deficient before the Japanese challenge and is unlikely to change, and that this lack of understanding is a threat to the success of the Free Trade Agreement.

Another Canadian concern is the extent of American ownership of Canadian businesses. There have been free trade agreements signed in many parts of the world, but none where one party owns almost half the other's economy. How will American subsidiaries in Canada respond to the free trade challenge? Many were established in the first place because Canadian tariffs made it too costly to compete in Canada by shipping products up from the United States. Now that the tariffs are being eliminated, what are American subsidiaries likely to do strategically? This is an enormously important question for Canada. It is treated in more detail in a later chapter, but it is useful to point out here that Canada's concern over foreign investment is really a reflection of the problem of size. Americans sometimes wonder why Canadians do not simply invest more in the United States rather than worrying about Americans investing in Canada. The facts are actually quite startling. American direct investment in Canada stands at Canadian $75.2 billion, while Canadian direct investment in the United States stands at Canadian $43.3 billion. Clearly Canadians invest proportionately more of their available investment capital in the United States than Americans do in Canada. To look at it another way, if two nations with similar per capita wealth each decide to invest 10 percent of their available capital in the other, and one nation is ten times bigger than the other, what is the result? Ten percent of the large nation's capital is equivalent to the small nation's entire wealth, while 10 percent of the small nation's capital makes only a 1 percent dent in the large nation. The investment problem is a size problem, not a reflection of Canada's lack of aggressiveness or competitiveness. Canada is investing proportionately more of its available capital in the United States than the United States is in Canada, but it is barely making a dent in the U.S. economy. The United States, on the other hand, with a less aggressive investment effort, owns almost half of Canada's manufacturing sector. In general, Canada has a ratio of foreign to domestic investment in its own economy eight times higher than does the United States. The behavior of foreign investors in Canada matters much more to the operation of the Canadian economy than does the behavior of foreign investors in the United States to the American economy. It is the relative size of the two economies that makes this so.

MOVING TOWARD INTERDEPENDENCE

It is useful to take stock before moving into new relationships and to try to understand one another's hopes, fears and aspirations. Canada's aspirations in signing the Free Trade Agreement were to transform and restructure its economy based on secure access to the American market. Product specialization, focussed research and increased trade, not only with the United States but with other nations as its competitiveness improves, were all part of Canada's hopes. The United States, on the other hand, was anxious to signal to the world that it was interested in free trade in both goods and services, and that it was other countries' unwillingness to open up their markets that constituted the real impediment to global trade liberalization. If the United States had been unable to reach a trade deal with Canada, its closest ally and neighbor, other nations would have presumed that the United States was trying to drive too hard and insensitive a bargain and that American insularity was the real impediment to global trade liberalization. A more direct American aspiration was to obtain better access to Canadian natural resources. Canada's hopes and aspirations were more practical and immediate than those of the United States, which had more to do with statesmanship. Canada's fears were more pressing, too: the fears of being swallowed up, losing its identity and sovereignty, losing jobs as subsidiaries in Canada switched strategies, and becoming painfully vulnerable to possible abrogation of the treaty. The U.S. fears were few and specific to those industries that might face loss of market share to Canadian competition.

The transition to interdependence is being undertaken by two nations with quite different hopes, fears and aspirations, and with relatively modest understanding of one another. Furthermore, the intensity of feeling about the relationship differs. It matters much more to Canadians than to Americans. But if the new relationship is to work, there needs to be an increase in understanding and trust between the two nations. As it is now, there is a measure of anti-Americanism in Canada's media that may well be due to the American media's penchant for relegating things Canadian to a mere postscript to the real news. A small percentage of Canadians see Americans as boastful, arrogant and insular, whereas Americans tend not to have an opinion about Canadians at all. These differences are played up in the media while the many similarities are not, all of which suggests that the way ahead may be rocky. Many Canadians are quite apprehensive about it, even among those who voted for the Free Trade Agreement. They feel dragged into it more by global economic developments than by any desire to proceed.

It is not difficult to understand Canada's reluctance, given the history of previous attempts at free trade. The inability of the two nations to proceed left Canada with a challenge to build a successful economy on its own behind a national boundary that made no economic sense at all. Most of Canada's population lives within a hundred miles of the border with the United States, like a long corridor. Since the failure of earlier negotiations made north-south trade and transportation rather costly, Canadians were faced with having to develop their own transportation and communication infrastructure along the corridor. It was a challenge that was essential to nationhood but difficult to tackle through the private-enterprise system alone. Canada's federal government had to get involved through crown corporations, and a mixed economy resulted that, despite its inefficiencies, got the job done rather effectively. Canadians are quite proud of these achievements and have quite different views on the merits of government involvement than do Americans. In general, Canadians trust government more than do Americans, in spite of their politicians. Canada's most right-wing political party, the Progressive Conservative party, is probably somewhat left of the American Democrats in its political outlook and perspective. There are not many genuine Republicans in Canada.

Now that the commercial barriers to trade are coming down, the inefficiencies of Canada's economy make restructuring essential. But it is going to be painful, and those most proud of Canada's forced achievements under a protectionist order are the least pleased about the new agreement. They see it as a betrayal of Canadian history. Others, however, take the view that Canada's achievements have given its people confidence to enter the new trade relationship without fear of being subsumed by the American juggernaut. From this perspective, Canada has a lot to contribute to the new "marriage": well-managed cities, an efficient medical system, generally better schools, and an ability to work with government in an essentially free-market economy. This latter characteristic may be more useful than Americans may think at first glance. Americans tend to have looked at the role of government in the economy ideologically, whereas Canadians, out of necessity, have looked at it practically. Issues such as environmental protection, research and development and the social accountability of corporations—important issues in the United States—may need the kind of creative business-government partnership Canadians understand. Not that Canada and the United States will necessarily be working together on these issues: the Free Trade Agreement does not envisage that. But a closer relationship, if cultivated well, will permit a much broader exchange of ideas and information than is now possible.

A final word for this opening chapter. Many Canadians are afraid that the road from independence to interdependence is too dangerous and may lead inexorably to dependence for the smaller nation. Others feel that it is possible to have the economic benefits of free trade without significant loss of cultural or political sovereignty. Of the latter group, many have doubts that they set aside because of the twin pressures of globalization and the knowledge revolution. The Free Trade Agreement now in effect has been designed to minimize the political and cultural risks to Canada. It has been structured to retain the sense of two separate markets, not one common market. Harmonization is not on the agenda. National treatment is the guiding principle. Trade disputes will be arbitrated by a binational panel. These are principles of interdependence and cooperation, not dependence and assimilation. They are important to Canadians, but to be effective they must first be understood. That is what subsequent chapters try to achieve.

NOTE

1. Walt Whitman, *Specimen Days* (New York: New American Library of World Literature, 1961), p. 220.

2

TWO MARKETS, NOT ONE

The Canada-U.S. Free Trade Agreement is much more than an agreement to reduce tariffs on goods traded between the two countries. It also includes agreements about investment, services and business travel and a mechanism to resolve trade disputes. It is much broader in scope than other free trade agreements negotiated under the GATT, particularly the 1960 European Free-Trade Area, the 1965 U.K.-Ireland Free-Trade Agreement, the 1983 Australia–New Zealand Closer Economic Relations Agreement, and the 1985 United States–Israel Agreement. In general, the broader an agreement, the greater the need for underlying principles to guide the negotiators in their task. It is important for both sides to understand the overall objectives clearly so that the agreement, when signed, will not be inconsistent with the desired direction.

There are two fundamental directions possible when entering into a trade agreement. One is to try to create a common market between the participating countries using common tariffs and common regulations, and the other is to try to retain separate markets with separate tariffs and regulations but with surer access for trade and investment. The Canada-U.S. Free Trade Agreement has clearly taken the latter course. This makes it quite different from the EEC with its common-market approach. Europe, through its 1992 initiative, is trying to take a huge step toward a single market with harmonized policies and regulations and even a common currency. Harmonization is not part of the Canada-U.S. Free Trade Agreement at all. The agreement uses the national-treatment principle instead. Rather than try to set common regulations to govern Canadian and American business environments, the agreement permits each country to retain whatever regulatory environment it wishes. However, the national-treatment principle requires each nation to avoid discriminating against the other nation's goods or firms. In effect, Canada agrees to treat American goods and firms the same way it treats its own, and America agrees to do the same for Canadian goods and firms. In this way each nation retains its own unique characteristics but learns to love its neighbor. A Canadian firm anxious to do business in the United States has to learn America's particular regulations and requirements but is assured that those regulations and requirements will not be any different for the American businesses it has to compete with. So it is for American firms anxious to do business in Canada. Canada does not agree to treat American firms the way they are treated in the United States. For example, bilingual labelling is a requirement to sell consumer goods in Canada. American firms anxious to sell consumer goods in Canada must pay the cost of bilingual labelling, even though in the United States bilingual labelling is not required. What the national-treatment principle assures them is that their Canadian competitors will face the same requirements. There will not be one set of rules for Canadians and a different, more exacting set for Americans. It is discrimination against the "foreigner" that the national-treatment principle forbids.

The distinction between national treatment and harmonization is a very important one. One might otherwise assume that Europe 1992 and the Canada-U.S. Free Trade Agreement are similar initiatives. They are, after all, both responses to the globalization challenge. But they are very different responses, and the difference is important to understand. It is essentially the difference between a common market and a free trade agreement, and that is a difference worth spending a little time on.

COMMON-MARKET PHILOSOPHY

Common markets normally begin with a desire for political union as well as economic reward. In the case of the EEC,[1] the vision of its early founders was to restructure Europe to reduce the possibility of yet another devastating war. Central to the vision was the reduction of national sovereignty and insularity, which were felt to be major contributors to distrust and hostility. The carrot was the prospect of access to a larger market with its attendant benefits in economies of scale and innovation. If all the major nations of Europe invested in and traded heavily with one another, went the vision, understanding would increase along with the standard of living, and the prospect of war would diminish. Out of the process would emerge Europe-wide institutions that would facilitate peaceful resolution of future problems.

The customs union or common market is much more than an economic arrangement. It sets out deliberately to create institutions that are political in nature. The technical way this is done is through the requirement that members of the customs union set a common external tariff against nonmembers (figure 2.1).

Figure 2.1
Customs Union or Common Market

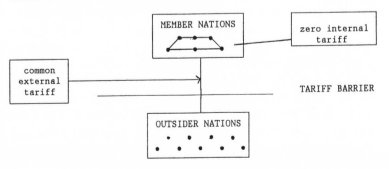

Member nations in a customs union enjoy tariff-free access to one another's markets—after an initial phase-in period—but when it comes to outsider nations, the member nations group together to set a common tariff policy. It is the common external tariff that distinguishes a customs union from a free trade agreement. It means that if an American firm wants to export into Europe, the tariff is the same whether it chooses to enter via France, Germany, Italy or any other EEC member nation. Who then sets the level of the common external tariff? Not any one nation-state, obviously. A new institution with powers broader than the nation-state must be established. In the case of the EEC it is the Common Market Commission under the Council of Ministers that sets policy for Europe. If this sounds like another level of bureaucracy and politics, that is exactly what it is. Europe has its own parliament. At first it was symbolic, had few powers and attracted few major political players. That is changing. The momentum of Europe 1992 has increased the interest of high-profile politicians in the European Parliament. But if the task is to set a common external tariff, does it not seem like institutional overkill to create a Council of Ministers, a Common Market Commission and a European Parliament? The answer, of course, is that much more was intended than the mere setting of a common external tariff, or, to be more precise, it was expected that the setting of a common external tariff would lead naturally to the need for common policies in other areas. For example, what about nontariff barriers to trade such as quotas, technical standards, subsidies to local firms and so on? More worrisome still, what about manipulation of exchange rates to enhance a nation's competitive position, or what about national tax systems that discriminate against imports? Who decides whether dumping is taking place? What about competition policy or patent policy?

The European view has been that if the common market is to work in the long run, nations must surrender their power to manipulate it to their own advantage. Nation-state power must give way to Europower. But when the issues involved are as significant as harmonization of currencies, tax policies and regulations, it is easy to see that an unelected European superpower could not reasonably do the job in the long term. The issues are too important to be dealt with by an unelected, nonrepresentative body—hence the European Parliament. To begin with, the member nations resisted the surrender of sovereignty to a central power and retained control of fiscal, monetary and regulatory policies. Hence while tariffs were systematically eliminated within the common market, inefficiencies grew from the unwillingness of member nations to harmonize their policies more fully. This was not altogether unexpected. A gradual process of adaptation was seen from the outset. But in the mid-1980s these nation-state–imposed barriers to the free movement of goods, services and people were estimated to be costing over $200 billion a year to the EEC as a whole. A white paper tabled by the European Commission in 1985 set out close to 300 measures to eliminate barriers and move aggressively toward a genuine single market by 1992. Globalization of markets, the Japanese challenge and the knowledge-based transformation of economic activity all played a role in creating a climate in Europe hospitable to accelerated change. The $200-billion annual waste could no longer be afforded.

The Vision of Europe 1992

The Europe 1992 initiative aims to restore Europe's competitiveness in relation to America and Japan by removing impediments to productivity and innovation. It is a bold initiative. Analysts think that achieving a single market in Europe will create around two million jobs, add between 5 and 7 percent to the community's gross domestic product (GDP) and lower consumer prices by 6 percent. Improvements in balance of payments and public-sector efficiency are also envisaged. The potential gains are huge. So are the risks and dangers. The barriers that the single-market initiative proposes to dismantle are of three kinds: physical, technical and fiscal.

Physical Barriers

Physical barriers are essentially the frontier border controls that halt the flow of people and goods and impose unnecessary cost and delay on European industry. It has been estimated that shipping by truck across Europe can take up to 50 percent longer than a trip of equivalent length within a single country. Border controls and their related paperwork are the culprit. The EEC proposes to tackle these issues through a mixture of streamlining and harmonizing. The idea is fewer regulations and similar regulations throughout the community. By late 1989 the community appeared to be making good progress on regulations affecting the movement of goods (except for health checks on plants and animals, which influence prices of farm products), but slow progress on a common passport. Free movement of people is being impeded by asylum seekers looking for a better standard of living, illegal immigrants and illegal shipments (guns and drugs). However, France, Germany and the Benelux countries are moving faster than the community as a whole toward creating a frontier-free zone.

Technical Barriers

Technical barriers refer to the various national rules that stop goods from being sold or capital from flowing, or firms of accountants or lawyers from setting up their offices across Europe. Technical barriers tend to restrict competition and make it difficult for firms to benefit from the potential scale economies of producing for a wider market. Among the technical barriers proposed for harmonizing are the following:

- Product standards, consumer and environmental regulations
- Health and safety standards
- Professional recognition and mobility
- Local-preference practices in government procurement
- Restrictions on capital movement

The agenda is bold indeed. The fundamental principles guiding discussion are again streamlining and harmonization, or at least mutual recognition of one another's standards. All visitors to Europe, for example, would be grateful if there were a single kind of wall plug. Harmonization is not going to be easy. Germany has a penchant for precise regulation. Many imported beers did not meet their purity standards, and some imported wines did not have enough alcohol in them to qualify as wines. The British sausage did not have enough meat in it to qualify as a sausage in Europe. These are silly illustrations, perhaps, but indicative of the scope for argument. Nevertheless, against the odds and to the surprise of the cynics, significant progress has been made, especially in the areas of environmental policy, professional mobility, consumer protection and product standards. There is a long way to go to reach the goal of a single market, but there is also a considerable momentum under way. On the cautious side, it is always the easier issues that get dealt with first, so the more contentious issues, like government procurement, are the ones next on the agenda.

At the same time changes in regulations that affect competition are going to face some opposition from business as well as from national governments. Most regulation affecting business has involved a cooperative effort on the part of business and government to set standards—initially in the interest of consumers in terms of quality and safety, but ultimately against consumers in terms of competition, choice and price. In Europe the balance seemed to tip over time against consumers, and Europe lost its competitiveness and innovativeness relative to Japan and America. Exposing a host of cozy national business-government regulatory arrangements to the comparative scrutiny of international examiners may well be a sobering process. It may illuminate one of the key reasons for the popular momentum of the 1992 initiative: that it is better for consumers. In most democratic nations producers have normally had the edge in influencing government regulation because they can organize more easily than consumers. Special-interest groups with their focus on single issues have also increased the quantity of inefficient regulation. So democracies, in general, have had a problem achieving a sensible balance in their regulatory practices. Europe is now moving toward a more efficiency-conscious regulatory system that is increasingly harmonized and consumer-friendly. The community has already achieved more in regulatory change than any nation-state is likely to have achieved through a deregulation blitz of its own, and it still has over two years to go.

Fiscal Barriers

Fiscal barriers are indirect taxes. The community has already adopted a common value-added tax (VAT) system, but different nations use different rates for different products, and some nations exempt some products entirely. The standard VAT rate varies from 12 percent in Luxembourg and Spain to 25 percent in Ireland. High rates on luxury goods reach 38 percent in Italy, and low rates on essential goods reach zero in the United Kingdom. The 1992 challenge is to tighten the degree of harmonization in VAT rates and coverage. The challenge is a difficult one, and discussion so far has made limited progress.

Overarching Objectives

It is clear by now that the single market is Europe 1992's main objective and harmonization is its main vehicle. During 1988 Jacques Delors, president of the European Commission, expressed the hope that "80% of economic, and perhaps social and tax legislation, could be of Community origin within ten years' time." Moves are afoot to achieve economic and monetary union through the creation of a single European currency and a central European bank, to achieve closer cooperation in making foreign policy and to achieve social improvement through a better specification of the rights of ordinary people.

The Sovereignty Barrier

Ideology plays an important part in politics, and nation-states have traditionally worked out for themselves how to apply ideology to economic activity. How this is to be done in a single European market is unclear. Will a "European" company be required to adopt German rules on worker participation in management? What will be the rights of unions in Europe? Will there be a minimum wage? Commenting on the struggle about ideology in the future of Europe, British prime minister Margaret Thatcher said in September 1988: "To try to suppress nationhood and concentrate power at the centre of a European conglomerate would be highly damaging. . . . Our aim should not be more and more detailed regulation from the centre. It should be to deregulate, to remove the constraints on trade and to open up." On balance, Europe 1992 seems to be reducing regulation, but the challenge to national sovereignty is unmistakable and deep. A less regulated Europe is offensive to those who believe that the capitalist system is dangerous without it. Their avenue for the development of a social safety net in Europe, the way things are emerging, will be the European Parliament rather than their own national governments. National sovereignty is likely to fight back over the next year or two, but it will have to fight intelligently. At present, national sovereignty in Europe is too easily associated with war, protectionism and inefficiency, all of which are out of favor as Europe tries to respond to the peaceful globalization of world markets.

FREE TRADE PHILOSOPHY

A free trade agreement attempts to capture the economic benefits of a customs union without the surrender of sovereign power to a central authority. It therefore has a similar economic objective to a customs union—the innovation and efficiency benefits of a large market—but a different political objective. The border between Canada and the United States has been a much more peaceful one than the European borders have been over the last century, and national sovereignty is not in the same disrepute here as it is in Europe. Hence the attempt in Europe to build a single market through harmonization of rules and policies and the establishment of greater central power is not what is being attempted between Canada and the United States. Americans, in fact, might not much object if a customs union were negotiated, but Canadians most certainly would. When the *Maclean's* poll asked Americans what they thought about adopting a common currency between Canada and the United States, 74 percent came out in favor, compared to 49 percent in Canada (which in turn was probably much higher than most Canadians expected). Asked about adopting a common policy of defense and foreign affairs, 73 percent of Americans supported the idea, and 60 percent of Canadians opposed it. It is not difficult to understand the different reactions. The United States, as the larger nation, might reasonably assume that it would retain much influence over the common currency or the common policy. Canada, as the smaller nation, could reasonably expect to lose influence to its larger neighbor. This is precisely why Canada and the United States are not planning to harmonize toward a single market. Canada was afraid that under harmonization it would be largely the Canadian regulations that would be swept away. So the Canada-U.S. Free Trade Agreement was built on national treatment rather than harmonization.

It was the choice of a free trade agreement rather than a customs union that made it possible to go the national-treatment route and thus retain two distinct markets but with improved reciprocal access. Free trade agreements do not involve common external tariffs (figure 2.2).

Because free trade agreements do not involve common external tariffs, no direct pressures arise to create common institutions to

Figure 2.2
Free Trade Agreement

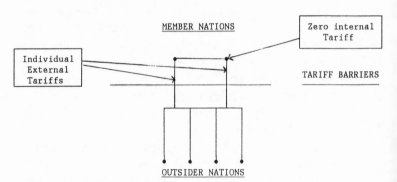

set and administer them. Tariff policy between the United States and other nations will continue to be handled by existing American government departments, as will Canadian tariff policy by the Canadian government. No new central institutions are envisaged in the agreement. Tariffs between Canada and the United States will be eliminated over time, but there is to be no single market. Outsider nations exporting to the United States will continue to pay the tariffs set by the American government. Outsider nations exporting to Canada will continue to pay the tariffs set by the Canadian government. Canadian tariffs are generally but not always higher than American tariffs. Several conclusions can be drawn from these simple observations:

1. American firms should be able to gain market share in Canada at the expense of other nations who still have to pay Canada's high tariffs.

2. Canadian firms should be able to gain market share in the United States at the expense of other nations, but since American tariffs are not as high, the Canadian competitive advantage will not be as great.

3. Canada and the United States could both gain from the agreement. It is not a zero-sum game. The two countries gain, not primarily at one another's expense, but at the expense of other nations.

4. Outsider nations will generally find the United States to be the lower-cost entry point to the North American market.

What then is to prevent a Japanese firm from exporting a product to the United States, paying the lower American tariff, and then transshipping the product to Canada under the Free Trade Agreement? If it were possible to do so, it would quickly destroy the usefulness of separate external tariff policies, which in turn are a fundamental feature of free trade agreements. So how do free trade agreements normally block this kind of trading arbitrage? They do it through local-content or rules-of-origin arrangements, and the Canada-U.S. Free Trade Agreement is no exception.

Rules of Origin for Goods

Chapter 3 of the agreement requires that goods must actually be made in Canada or the United States in order to qualify for tariff-free treatment. Foreign-made goods do not fall under the agreement at all. However, in an era of globalization, many products are in fact assembled from components made in many parts of the world. The agreement uses 50 percent as the qualifying degree of local content for "mixed products." At least 50 percent of the manufacturing cost of a product has to be accounted for in Canada and/or the United States before the product qualifies for duty-free treatment.

Canada had a particular difficulty with clothing and textiles when it came to local content. Canada's clothing industry has competed over the past decade by buying fabrics offshore to differentiate their clothing from American competitors, who, in general, used American fabrics. Canadian clothing manufacturers wanted tariff-free access to the American market for their apparel made in Canada from offshore fabrics. The American textile industry did not want Canadian apparel makers to have that loophole. American textile producers were concerned that if the Canadians succeeded with their proposed strategy, American apparel makers might follow suit. In their view, apparel made from offshore textiles should not qualify under the Free Trade Agreement. Canadian apparel makers, of course, disagreed, claiming that if they had to buy fabrics in Canada or the United States, they would lose their competitive edge. Furthermore, the Canadian textile producers disagreed with the Canadian apparel makers. They faced their own quite different set of problems. They had to limit their range of output to certain popular fabrics because the Canadian market was not big enough for them to make a full line efficiently. They therefore did not make many of the more sophisticated fabrics. However, they saw in the Free Trade Agreement a chance to break out of the small-market syndrome they were in. They began buying market position in the United States and quickly came to the same view as American textile manufacturers.

The issue may almost have scuttled the agreement. The textile lobby is very strong in the United States, and negotiators in Canada felt that if they did not compromise on Canadian apparel exports, the agreement might be derailed. Whether they were right in their judgment may never be known, but a compromise was built into chapter 3 of the agreement giving clothing made from offshore textiles a duty-free quota in each market. The way it works is that clothing made from offshore, nonwoolen fabrics can enter the United States duty-free up to 50 million equivalent square yards and can enter Canada duty-free up to 10.5 million equivalent square yards. A separate quota was developed for woolen fabrics.

This illustration is given not only to point out some of the complications and challenges that arise in trade negotiations, but also to underline how seriously local-content arrangements are taken in free trade agreements. As a rule, they do not arise in customs unions because of the common external tariff. However, some talk of local content or rules of origin may surface during the Europe 1992 initiative for a quite different reason. The EEC has from time to time taken antidumping action against outside nations or has put quotas on, say, Japanese cars. Having done so, it needs to say what a Japanese car is. What about a Honda made in the United Kingdom as part of the Honda-Rover joint venture? The point is that a firm facing antidumping charges or quotas may readily shift its shipments to an affiliate plant in another country. For example, a Japanese videocassette recorder (VCR) producer may have a plant in South Korea. If quotas are put on Japanese VCRs, the Japanese producer may simply ship VCRs beyond his quota from South Korea. Furthermore, the South Korean plant may be only an assembly operation, with all the key parts coming from Japan. These are called screwdriver plants. The EEC has taken the position that screwdriver plants are just an inexpensive way of circumventing trade laws and has insisted on at least 40 percent local content before the product is deemed to come from the country where it is located. So local-content rules do arise in the EEC, but for quite different and somewhat less direct reasons.

Eliminating Internal Tariffs

One thing customs unions and free trade agreements do have in common is the phased elimination of tariffs between the participating nations. Tariff elimination is, of course, the central purpose of the exercise; most other rules are put in place to prevent the erection of substitute barriers once the tariffs have been eliminated. In most trade agreements, including the EEC, tariffs are eliminated gradually to give firms time to adjust to the new realities. Adjustment time was needed in Canada, not for all industries, but for most. A number of Canadian industries—steel, automotive, pulp and paper, wood products and so on—were quite competitive in the United States when free trade began in 1989, but many others were not.

Take major appliances as an example. Canadian appliance manufacturers had been producing the full range of refrigerators, ranges, washers, dryers and dishwashers for the Canadian market. The Canadian market was not big enough to allow the firms to get the maximum available economies of scale, so their American competitors were more efficient. However, the tariff permitted the Canadian firms to function profitably by keeping out the more efficient American producers. In 1983, when the Canadian tariff on most appliances was 20 percent and the Canadian dollar was worth seventy to seventy-five cents in U.S. currency, the Canadian appliance producers were well insulated from American competition. By 1989, with the tariff down to 12 percent—courtesy of the Tokyo round of the GATT—and the Canadian dollar between eighty and eighty-five cents, the Canadian producers were very vulnerable to the more efficient American producers.

Take away the 12 percent tariff immediately in 1989, and the Canadian producers are in serious and immediate trouble: hence the case for gradual tariff removal under the Free Trade Agreement. But first we have to ask the question, why have the Canadian producers not moved independently to position themselves better for free trade? Why hasn't there been a shakeout in Canada? If Canadian firms could become more efficient by getting bigger, why have there not been any buyouts or joint ventures? The reason is that the big three appliance producers in Canada are all foreign-owned: in fact, they were all American-owned until Electrolux bought out White Consolidated Industries (WCI). The other two are owned by General Electric (GE) and Whirlpool. The subsidiaries in Canada were simply not for sale even if they were not doing all that well. It was not only that their parents had deep pockets; it was also that Canada's rules about foreign investment extended to sales of foreign subsidiaries to other parents for most of the 1980's. In fact, when WCI bought Westinghouse's appliance division in 1975, it was blocked by Canada's Foreign Investment Review Agency from taking control of Westinghouse Canada's appliance division; it had to be sold to a Canadian buyer. One result of this policy was to make it much more difficult for industries in Canada to restructure as global competition intensified. Canada's foreign investment policies were modified in the late 1980's, and article 1607 of the Canada-U.S. Free Trade Agreement exempted acquisitions of subsidiaries by other foreign-owned firms from the Canadian review process.

Nevertheless, when the Free Trade Agreement was signed, Canada was faced with a number of industries, like the major-appliance industry, that were going to have to restructure in order to be competitive in a tariff-free environment. It was necessary to give them time to adjust. As a result, the free trade negotiators involved business and industry representatives in the negotiating process as far as determining the speed with which tariffs should decline. Three options were made available, and business and industry representatives on both sides of the border tried to agree on one of the three. The options were immediate full tariff removal on January 1, 1989; gradual tariff removal over five years in equal annual installments beginning January 1, 1989; and gradual tariff removal over ten years on the same basis. The all-at-once option involved industries with minor adjustment problems on both sides. The following list of industries and products on which tariffs have now been eliminated constitutes about 15 percent of all dutiable goods traded between Canada and the United States.

Industries and Products on Which Tariffs Were Eliminated on January 1, 1989

Airbrakes for railroad cars	Pork (some)
Animal feeds	Skates
Computer and related equipment	Skis
Ferro alloys	Unprocessed fish (some)
Fur and fur garments	Unwrought aluminum
Leather	Vending machines and parts
Motorcycles	Warranty repairs
Needles	Whiskey
Papermaking machinery (some)	Yeast

A further 35 percent of dutiable U.S.-Canada trade is represented by the products and industries placed on the five-year tariff-removal track. On these, tariffs are to be reduced in 20 percent annual installments, with the first cut occurring on January 1, 1989.

Industries and Products on Which Tariffs Will Be Eliminated over Five Years

Aftermarket auto parts	Meats (some, including lamb)
Chemicals, including resins, drugs and cosmetics	Paints
	Paper and paper products
Explosives	Printed matter
Furniture	Subway cars
Hardwood plywood	Telecommunication equipment
Machinery (most)	

The remaining 50 percent of dutiable trade has been placed on the ten-year tariff-reduction track ending on January 1, 1998. If the hopes of the negotiators are fulfilled in the reality, Canada and the United States will enter the next millennium with no artificial impediments to their trade and investment. Many things will have to go right for this dream to be realized, but it is an exciting and timely initiative. The ten-year list of products and industries—where significant adjustment needs were anticipated in one country or the other—is as follows:

Industries and Products on Which Tariffs Will Be Eliminated Over Ten Years

Agricultural products (most)	Softwood plywood
Appliances	Steel
Beef	Textiles and apparel
Pleasure craft	Tires
Railcars	

Getting the Agreement Signed in the United States

President Reagan agreed to put the agreement on the fast-track process for congressional approval. The agreement and its implementing legislation were formally tabled in the U.S. Congress in the spring of 1988. Under the fast-track process, up to ninety "sitting days" were allowed to achieve congressional approval—sixty days in the House of Representatives and thirty days in the Senate. At the end of the process, a yes/no vote was called on both the agreement and the enabling legislation. Under the fast-track provisions, Congress was not allowed to dismember the agreement and reject particular clauses. This was important to the negotiators because all agreements of this magnitude involve many compromises on both sides, and the chances of getting the agreement through would be slim indeed if politicians could alter it clause by clause. The agreement had either to be accepted as negotiated or rejected. Senate approval was given on September 19, 1988. A six-month termination clause was attached to it, however, and this worried Canadians because of the greater adjustment problem they faced. It was not that Congress especially wanted a six-month termination clause on the agreement. The termination clause was a direct effect of using the fast-track process. All fast-track congressional decisions have six-month termination clauses attached to them, presumably to limit the potential cost of decisions made in haste. Canadians are anxious to alter the six-month termination clause, and Americans seem willing to oblige. Whether a way can be found remains to be seen.

Getting the Agreement Signed in Canada

Approval in Canada was expected to be easier than in America because of Prime Minister Brian Mulroney's massive majority in the House of Commons. Canada utilizes a parliamentary form of democracy inherited from its British ties, and legislation is enacted by majority vote in the House. As expected, Prime Minister Mulroney used the majority held by his Progressive Conservative party to shepherd the agreement and its enabling legislation through the House of Commons and on to the Senate for approval by July 1988. Here it hit a roadblock. The Senate, in Canada, is not an elected body. Senators are appointed for life by the prime minister. Since the opposition Liberal party had been in power for most of the last fifteen years, Liberal political sentiment dominated the Senate. The Honourable John Turner, leader of the Liberal party, invited his Liberal colleagues in the Senate to block the Free Trade Agreement, and they did. Because it is an unelected body, the Senate cannot reject legislation emanating from the House of Commons, but it can delay it, usually by requesting amendments. Since the terms of the agreement were set to take effect on January 1, 1989, both nations were expected to approve the enabling legislation before that date. The Canadian Senate could clearly have delayed it well beyond that. A general election had to be called to break the impasse, which was precisely what the Liberal leaders hoped for. The election turned into a passionate debate on free trade, on which the next chapter will comment further, but when the votes were finally counted, Mulroney's Progressive Conservatives still had their majority, albeit significantly reduced. As a result, the agreement and its enabling legislation were reintroduced into the House of Commons in December 1988 and quickly approved. The Senate was not prepared to oppose the voice of the people and promptly fell into line. Canadian approval made the January 1, 1989, deadline, but only just.

SPECIAL PROVISIONS OF THE AGREEMENT

The agreement contained many special provisions: some for specific industries like agriculture, automotive, energy and financial services, and others for such issues as government procurement (little progress here), border measures and technical barriers. These areas are presented in some detail in appendix B for readers with a special interest in them. The remainder of this chapter will concentrate on three areas that were particularly important to one or both countries: exempting one another from emergency protectionist measures aimed at other countries, establishing a new process for resolving trade disputes, and facilitating trade in services.

American Protectionism Not Aimed at Canada

As global competition hit the American market and the U.S. trade deficit climbed sharply in the 1980s, there were repeated calls for protectionism. Most of the protectionism was aimed at Japan and the Far East and took the form of imposing "voluntary" quotas on nations that were thought to be trading unfairly. Unfair trade involved anything from price dumping to subsidizing exports and limiting access to one's own markets. The United States began to argue for greater trade reciprocity and a more level playing field, and Canadians began to get nervous about the consequences. Under GATT rules the United States could take action under the emergency provisions of article XIX because it faced a surge in imports, but it could not apply protectionist initiatives against targeted nations—all GATT nations have to be treated alike. Canadians saw a risk of being sideswiped by U.S. "emergency" legislation aimed at other nations' unfair trade practices that Canadians did not engage in.

The reason that this issue was so important to Canadians is that Canada is a trading nation to a far greater degree than the United States or Japan. Exports represent 28 percent of GDP in Canada, compared to 7 percent in the United States. Furthermore, the United States is the destination for about 80 percent of Canada's exports. Any move that might limit Canada's access to the U.S. market is a cause for deep concern in Canada. As a result, chapter 11 of the Canada-U.S. Free Trade Agreement exempts both nations from emergency protectionist action by the other. A free trade agreement was almost the only way to achieve such an exemption and stay within GATT rules. Of course, where the import surge is being caused by the other nation, the exemption does not apply. At the same time, when the exemption does apply, the nation exempted is not supposed to rush in and take undue advantage of the situation. While the exemption clause in the agreement applies naturally to both Canada and the United States, it is to Canada that it really matters.

Settling Disputes: The Binational Panel

The existing trade laws of each nation are not superseded by the Free Trade Agreement. Unfair trade laws on dumping and subsidization apply in both countries but tend to be a greater irritant to Canadian firms than to American firms. One reason for this, of course, is that exports are a greater percentage of corporate sales in Canada than in the United States, and this situation will be accentuated if the Free Trade Agreement succeeds. Another reason is the way the process is managed in the two countries: Canadians use a formal judicial process, while Americans use a faster administrative process. Canadian firms sometimes feel intimidated by U.S. trade laws because of the ease with which their American competitors can set a dumping inquiry in motion when the only evidence is that the Canadian firm is winning market share. Anti-dumping investigators arrive at the Canadian company's doorstep on a fishing expedition for evidence, and failure to comply with their request for data leads to a presumption of guilt. Two pieces of evidence are needed to establish dumping: first, that the exporter is selling abroad below his domestic price, and second, that he is causing injury to local firms. Canadian firms often have to use lower prices in the United States in order to compete and sometimes get accused of dumping even though their prices are not below prevailing U.S. prices. It would not be difficult to imagine the concern in Canada if the Free Trade Agreement had been approved without some way of taking the "political" risk out of trade. Again, it is useful to remember that a Canadian firm with equal market shares in Canada and the United States would have over 90 percent of its sales in the American market. If Canada were to have improved access to the American market through free trade, how secure would that access be? How vulnerable would Canada be to the vagaries of American trade law administration? This issue was so important to Canada that on September 23, 1987, Canadian negotiators broke off the talks over it and returned to Canada, saying, "The free trade talks are dead."

But if Canadian firms are neither dumping nor subsidizing exports, why should they be worried about American trade laws? Is this the nervousness of the guilty? Do Canadians want access to the American market without the normal procedures to prevent unfair trade? Not at all. What Canada pressed for was a procedure for joint resolution of disputes. Prior to the Free Trade Agreement a dispute over Canadian exports to the United States would be adjudicated by an American body, the International Trade Commission, while disputes over American trade with Canada would be handled by the Canadian Import Tribunal. There have been a number of high-profile disputes in the past—Canadian softwood lumber and cedar shakes and shingles, for example—that have raised serious concerns about what really constitutes a subsidy. In the softwood lumber dispute American officials claimed that Canada was subsidizing its lumber industry through low stumpage fees—the fees levied to chop down a tree. In Canada the government owns vast wooded areas and controls the rate at which trees are taken and the rate at which reforestation occurs. In the United States the land is privately owned and privately managed, albeit with government regulations. Private ownership affects the price of the land, and that plus profit margins sets the stumpage fee. Canada's forests were being operated so that the stumpage fees provided the funds for reforestation and general management. The Canadian stumpage fee was much lower than the American stumpage fee, and American officials charged Canada with subsidizing exports. Since there was no overt subsidy payment by government in Canada, Canadians did not like this judgment. It appeared that American talk of level playing fields meant their playing field. Eventually, the issue was defused by Canada imposing a 15 percent export tax on softwood lumber in order to avoid American countervailing duties. As it turned out, Canadian export volumes on softwood lumber were not much affected by the export tax, but prices to American users went up. While the immediate problem was resolved, the broader issue of what really constitutes a subsidy was not. It was not resolved during the free trade negotiations either.

As the negotiations proceeded, the Canadian side became more and more convinced that without an acceptable mechanism for resolving trade disputes Canada would be too vulnerable under the Free Trade Agreement. Canada's view of an acceptable mechanism was that disputes should be jointly resolved and binding on both sides. American negotiators agreed to joint determination, that is, a binational panel, but not to making the panel's judgments binding. There was a deep reluctance in the United States to having domestic laws overridden by an unelected body not under American control. Canada was not willing to enter into the Free Trade Agreement without a binational panel with binding powers. This was the dilemma that broke up the talks and almost scuttled the agreement.

It required direct involvement of senior political figures from both countries to break the impasse. The initiative came from the United States. U.S. Treasury Secretary James Baker and U.S. Trade Representative Clayton Yeutter convened a meeting in Washington on September 28 with Canada's Michael Wilson, minister of finance, and Pat Carney, minister of trade, and their respective advisors. The meeting failed to provide the assurances Canadians needed. It appeared that the impasse was too deep. On October 1 Prime Minister Mulroney called a meeting of provincial leaders in Canada for the next day to explain why negotiations had been terminated. Later that day Treasury Secretary Baker phoned Ottawa offering to resume talks based on a significant shift in the American position on dispute resolution. After a brief flurry of meetings on October 2 and 3 the impasse was broken—albeit not until 11:50 P.M. The new binational panel's decisions were to be binding, more or less. Canadian lawyers poring over the details subsequently claimed to be able to drive trucks through the loopholes, but then lawyers seem to be able to drive trucks through most things.

What was eventually set up was a five-person panel with two Americans, two Canadians and a fifth member to be agreed on by the other four or chosen at random from an approved list of "panelists." The idea was that each nation would have an acceptable list of potential panelists and that a new panel would be convoked to hear each issue referred. Issues will be referred when either side feels that the other has made an unfair judgment under its trade laws. In this sense the binational panel does not replace existing trade law but becomes a final "court of appeal." Its decisions are expected to be followed but are not binding in the technical sense. There is a potential cost to not following them.

The binational dispute-settlement process is expected to accomplish three things:

1. Development of a set of mutually agreed rules about what constitutes dumping and subsidies, expected to be a five-to-seven-year process that will take the rather vague GATT definitions as a starting point

2. Provision of a binational panel review of domestic decisions under antidumping and countervailing duty laws when required

3. Provision of a bilateral review of any changes to either nation's trade laws to see that the changes are consistent with the GATT and with the objectives of the agreement

These three things over time should put a good deal more security and predictability into Canada-U.S. trade. Firms caught breaking trade laws will still be challenged, but as the rules become clearer, they will at least know that they are breaking trade laws and will deserve what they get. Also, with both nations working together on the rules, it is likely that a more thoughtful set of rules will emerge, and that the level playing field will not be too one-sided.

Trade in Services

The service sector of developed economies is growing rapidly at the expense of the manufacturing sector, but it is not displacing it. Many services, such as transportation, insurance, financing, product design and engineering, accounting, retailing and after-sales service, are related to manufacturing. Some are performed in-house by large manufacturers and some are purchased on the open market. During the 1980's, as U.S. trade deficits worsened, Americans began to realize that their competitiveness in services was better than their competitiveness in goods, but that trade barriers were falling primarily in goods. In other words, global markets were opening up in goods, where the United States was relatively weak, but not in services, where it was relatively strong. The problem was that barriers to trade in services were different kinds of barriers and were difficult even to get onto the GATT agenda. Most barriers consisted of discriminatory rules against foreigners and their rights to establish operations. (Just think of the opportunity if the United States could export lawyers). Trade in services was important to Americans. It was felt that success in dealing with it in the Canada-U.S. trade negotiations would enhance American efforts to get it onto the agenda of the Uruguay round of the GATT and provide an example of how to deal with it there. Indeed, the issue is successfully on the GATT agenda, and there is a distinct possibility that the Canada-U.S. accord will be the basis for initial discussion in Uruguay.

Article 1401 in the agreement applies the nondiscriminatory principle of national treatment to trade in services. Canada and the

United States have agreed not to discriminate against one another's service companies. They are to be treated the same. However, it is worth repeating that national treatment does not imply harmonization of rules. Canada may evolve quite different regulations for its service sector than the United States, but those regulations will be applied in a similar way to both Canadian and American firms. Other sections of the agreement go on to liberalize the climate for moving people across the border and for direct investment. These clauses are important for trade in services because services are usually embodied in people and their knowledge, and investment freedom affects the right to establish.

Under chapter 15 of the agreement both nations agree to adjust their immigration rules to facilitate business travel. Professionals will be able to cross the border more easily, and firms will be able to transfer people more easily to their subsidiaries in the other country. On the investment side, the national-treatment principle is applied under article 1602 to all new businesses. Americans can set up new businesses in Canada without a review process and without having to make commitments about local content and exports or other matters. When it comes to takeovers of existing businesses, however, Canada's review process still applies, but only on large acquisitions. By 1992 only acquisitions above $150 million Canadian dollars will be reviewed. Provision is also made that disputes over investment issues may be referred to the dispute-settlement process under the agreement.

CONCLUSION

The Canada-U.S. Free Trade Agreement is strikingly different from the Europe 1992 initiative. Unlike the EEC, Canada and the United States are not trying to create a single market and are not trying to harmonize policies and regulations. We may, of course, end up harmonizing to a point if both countries find it desirable, but the agreement does not require it. Canada and the United States are not setting up strong central institutions to administer the agreement. The binational panel is more like a judicial appendage to existing institutions. Compared to the EEC, there is very little surrender of national sovereignty envisaged in the Canada-U.S. Free Trade Agreement. Making it work is going to depend on cooperation and understanding rather than a shift of legislative power to central institutions. For nations in Europe, with their different languages and customs and their history of hostilities over many centuries, it is likely that nothing short of a common market with its attendant surrendering of national sovereignty would have worked. Whether Canada and the United States can make a free trade agreement work on the basis of interdependence of equals remains to be seen.

Much will depend on how businesses adapt to the free trade era, particularly American businesses with subsidiaries in Canada. Will their strategies in Europe be different from their strategies in Canada? Will they see one market between Canada and the United States, or two? Most Canadian subsidiaries of American firms operated fairly independently before the Free Trade Agreement was signed because, by and large, they concentrated on the Canadian market. If they are to gain the efficiency benefits of free trade, Canadian subsidiaries are going to have to become international players in their own right. That will mean some loss of independence. There will be a greater need for coordination between parents and subsidiaries. Will the loss of subsidiary independence lead to interdependence in the spirit of the Free Trade Agreement or to dependence under the centralizing ethos of globalization? Chapters 4 and 5 address this issue from the standpoint of parents and subsidiaries, respectively. The next chapter deals with some of the ideological aspects of free trade, particularly those dealing with the consequences of protectionism, such as internal balkanization, adversarial labor relations, government intervention in the economy and the challenge to national confidence.

NOTE

1. There were originally six nations involved in the founding of the EEC: Belgium, France, Germany, Italy, Luxembourg and the Netherlands. These six nations signed the initial Treaty of Paris in 1952 that led to the successful

European Coal and Steel Community. They subsequently signed the Treaty of Rome in 1957 to establish a full customs union and found the EEC. The EEC has since been joined by the United Kingdom, Denmark and Ireland (1973), Greece (1981) and Portugal and Spain (1986). The addition of Portugal and Spain increased membership in the community to twelve nations with over 320 million people.

3

OVERCOMING THE LEGACY OF PROTECTIONISM

The Canada-U.S. Free Trade Agreement is about trade and economics rather than ideology, but it would have been difficult to reach that conclusion while listening to the rhetoric of Canada's 1988 general election. The trade unions opposed the agreement because they claimed that it would cost jobs. American parent companies would shut down their Canadian subsidiaries and supply the Canadian market from American facilities. Church groups opposed it because it would lead to an excessively competitive society in which the poor and the handicapped would be left behind. Politicians opposed it because it would limit regional subsidies and scuttle national support programs like medicare. Political scientists opposed it because of the threat to national sovereignty—the fear of Canada becoming the fifty-first state. The arts community opposed it as a betrayal of Canada and its history. Nobody really opposed reducing tariffs, which was the agreement's main purpose. The opposition was focussed on where free trade might lead. It was the ideological danger that galvanized the opposition.

Actually, the 1988 federal election in Canada started out rather quietly with the incumbent party defending its record of economic growth and the opposition parties trying to stake out populist middle-ground positions. The ruling Progressive Conservatives tried to position the Free Trade Agreement as just one part of their economic program for the future. However, when John Turner, leader of the opposition, charged Mulroney in a nationally televised political debate with "selling out Canada," the election campaign changed course dramatically. The public got aroused. Many expressed their fears about the agreement, while others asked for information so they could reach their own conclusions. What emerged was an ideological debate about the kind of society people wanted. In order to understand the elements of that debate, it is useful to look first at the state Canada was in before the agreement—to examine, if you will, the legacy of protectionism.

THE LEGACY OF PROTECTIONISM

Protecting one's markets from the inroads of foreign competition seems such an attractive proposition when first made. It is not difficult to explain that imports reduce domestic employment. Nor is it difficult to persuade people that foreigners with their strange customs, low wage rates and weak social programs are inherently unfair competitors. Add to these arguments the notion that home-grown businesses need time to become more competitive, and tariff protection is easy to justify. In Canada's case there was yet another argument. Forced by history to build a national economy east-west along a narrow corridor, it could not possibly compete with the much larger American economy. Tariffs against American imports were essential to stimulate investment. They were, in fact, the basis for massive American investment in Canada to produce behind the Canadian tariff wall. They led directly to the heavy U.S. ownership of Canadian business that has worried many Canadians.

But protectionism breeds deeper problems than foreign ownership. It leads to internal balkanization, excessive regulation, greater influence for labor unions and greater power for government. The resulting economy is not only inefficient, it often lacks the spark of challenge and innovation. It is a stagnant pond. Research and development cannot thrive in it. Originality flounders under a blanket of egalitarianism. Let us examine these issues one at a time so that we can come to grips with the attitudinal changes free trade is going to require.

Internal Balkanization

If a nation decides that protectionism is an appropriate national policy, what is to stop states or provinces within that nation also adopting it? Why should protectionism stop at the national border? These are vexing questions for those who would wrap their support for protectionism in the nationalist flag. Canada's experience was that protectionism did not stop at the national border; provinces began erecting protectionist measures of their own. Their logic was deceptively simple. The provinces of Ontario and Quebec have historically been Canada's chief manufacturing provinces and chief suppliers of manufactured goods to the Maritime and Prairie provinces. Since national protectionism (that is, tariffs) made it more expensive to import from the United States, a dependency relationship grew between the central provinces and the eastern and western ones. It was no great leap of logic for the noncentral provinces to decide that their manufacturers just needed time to become competitive with Ontario and Quebec. They did not have the jurisdiction to impose tariffs, of course, so they had to resort to more subtle means of protectionism. Provincial governments began to give preference to in-province suppliers in their purchasing; businesses were offered capital incentives to locate facilities in other provinces; some products were not allowed to be sold in a province unless they were made there.

Breweries became the classic example of a balkanized industry in Canada. Every province in Canada required breweries to locate a plant in the province in order to sell beer there, and most provincial governments controlled the retailing of all alcoholic beverages. The result was a proliferation of small breweries and higher prices for beer. Expose this cozy arrangement to the competitive blast of free trade with the giant American breweries, and there is no way it can survive. As a result, the brewing industry was exempted from the Free Trade Agreement. It is going to take some time before Canadian breweries will be prepared for more open competition.

Relations between the provinces and the federal government in Canada have not been all that good under protectionism, as one might expect. Jurisdictional arguments have been endless. The story is often told of the international essay competition on the life of the elephant in which the British entrant wrote on "The History of the Elephant"; the French entrant on "The Love Life of the Elephant"; the German on "The Metabolism of the Elephant"; the American on "How to Build Bigger and Better Elephants"; and the Canadian on "The Elephant, a Federal or Provincial Responsibility." Given the elephant-and-mouse portrait on the wall of the Canadian negotiator's office, it might seem that Canadians have a preoccupation with elephants. Canadians certainly have a preoccupation with federal-provincial disputes, most of which are about the distribution rather than the creation of wealth. Protectionism has done much to foster a disputational climate by holding in check the outside common challenge. Once the process of balkanization gets under way, even provinces like Ontario that oppose it in principle find themselves taking part. If one province discriminates, others respond. A province that does not discriminate ends up losing market share.

The wine industry in Ontario is a case in point. It has been regulated directly by the Ontario government for many years. Ontario wineries in 1986 were required to purchase 85 percent of their grape requirements in Ontario, where it was difficult and costly to grow the better varieties that make for good wine. Furthermore, the price of the grapes was set by the grape growers' marketing board at levels well above world prices. The wineries, of course, would have been unable to compete with imported wines or out-of-province wines as long as they were regulated into buying expensive Ontario grapes. To help them to compete, a compensating benefit was granted to the wineries by the Liquor Control Board of Ontario, which controlled the pricing and distribution of wines in the province. The benefit took the form of a lower retail markup for Ontario wines. Imported wines at one stage were marked up 125 percent, compared to 105 percent for out-of-province wines and 58 percent for Ontario wines. In one swoop the principle of protectionism was applied first to foreigners and then to other Canadians, albeit at a lower rate. The retail markup differentials were calculated to allow Ontario wineries to operate profitably despite the requirement to purchase high-cost Ontario grapes. The wine industry in Ontario was another example of a cozy regulatory arrangement in which the fledgling local industry was supported at the expense of consumer prices.

Things changed dramatically, however, when the Canada-U.S. Free Trade Agreement was signed. Chapter 3 of the agreement called for the elimination of the differential markup on imported wines over seven years, with half of it to be eliminated in two years. This immediately set in motion pressures in Canada to eliminate the interprovincial differential markups as well. Free trade, it seems, is an antidote to balkanization. As it turned out, the initialling of the Free Trade Agreement on October 4, 1987, was followed by a ruling under the GATT that Canada's differential markups on imported wines contravened GATT principles. The ruling was not altogether unexpected in Canada, and there was some speculation that Canada's trade negotiators cannily sacrificed the wine industry in the free trade talks to win exemption for the brewing industry, knowing full well that the GATT ruling would require Canada to stop discriminating against imported wines anyway or face possible retaliation. Be that as it may, the Free Trade Agreement came as quite a shock to the comfortable Ontario wine industry. Provincial politicians faced a dilemma. Ontario had embraced international competitiveness with the signing of the Free Trade Agreement, but its wine industry was still trapped in a web of protectionist regulations. Compensation was a possibility, but that soon turned into a federal-provincial issue of whose budget should pay it. Meanwhile, the previously cordial relationships between the wineries and the grape growers in Ontario collapsed, as the wineries quickly pointed out that they could not compete internationally as long as they were forced to buy Ontario grapes. The wineries wanted the grape-buying regulations dismantled, and the grape growers were predictably upset.

Dismantling protective local arrangements that have grown up without the discipline of international competition is one of the things free trade does well. However, it does not do it without pain, and it is never an easy task to explain to people who are hurting that pain is good for them. When it comes to changing the attitudes and mind-sets that Canadians have developed over decades of protectionism, the challenge is a difficult one indeed. People have to be persuaded to take a leap of faith, and leaps of faith are not in vogue in Canada or in most other countries. We deal with this issue later in the chapter, but first let us look at some of the other fruits of protectionism.

Trade Union Power

The Canada-U.S. Free Trade Agreement is going to erode union power in Canada for the same reasons the Japanese challenge has eroded union power in America. When the American economy was more efficient and more innovative than other economies in the world, its businesses were protected from international competition largely by their own superior performance. In those circumstances it was difficult not to agree with union demands for higher wages, shorter hours or more rigid shopfloor rules. The costs could easily be passed on to the consumer without significant loss of market share to foreign competitors. Negotiators argued about the appropriate division of profit between capital and labor. Behind all the rhetoric, negotiators would often, in practice, quietly agree to a deal that the union was confident that workers would accept and that the management was confident could be recouped in higher prices. The loser was the consumer. Enter Japanese competition, and suddenly the rules of the negotiating game changed. The efficiency and innovativeness of American industry had eroded to the point that foreign producers became competitive. The thrust of labor negotiations had to change from how to divide the profit to how to regain market share. Managements began to press for wage rollbacks on the basis that previous generous settlements were the reason for America's competitive weakness. Unions cooperated to a degree because the alternative was not higher prices but loss of jobs to foreign competitors. Consumers benefited not only from lower prices but also from better quality. But then consumers usually do benefit from foreign competition; it is existing establishments that do not, and these establishments—business and labor—will not act in the best interest of consumers as often without the pressure of foreign competition.

When it came to support for the Free Trade Agreement, there was a split in Canada between business leaders and union leaders. With few exceptions business leaders supported free trade, while the Canadian Labour Congress opposed it vigorously. Strangely, this was not the case when it came to dealing with Japanese competition in the Canadian auto market. A joint management-labor task force unitedly urged the Canadian government to force high–local-content rules on the Japanese carmakers as a condition of market entry. In other words, Japanese cars would have to achieve significant Canadian content to be eligible to be sold in Canada. The idea of free trade was conveniently set aside by the task force. The Canadian government, to its credit, did not accept the recommendation. It seems that while business supports free trade and international competition in general, if it is possible to exempt one's own industry from it, that is a different matter.

To be fair, the auto industry in Canada did require special treatment under the Free Trade Agreement because of the existence of the 1965 Auto Pact. Under the pact cars and original equipment parts could flow duty free between Canada and the United States. However, only businesses could import tariff free; individuals could not. Since the major North American auto companies were all U.S.-owned, special arrangements were built into the pact to require a stated level of Canadian assembly and Canadian content. Under the Auto Pact the Canadian auto industry did not have to compete with its U.S. counterpart to achieve its stated share of business activity. The pact required Canadian assembly and Canadian content regardless of comparative productivity performance. However, the Canadian auto industry did perform well, with the help of a weak Canadian dollar, and by 1989 had achieved a sizeable trade surplus with the United States.

Once the free trade debate got under way, the Canadian Auto Workers were quick to point out that free trade threatened the Auto Pact. They were right, of course. The threat was in the simple fact that tariff removal would take away the need for the pact. Their main complaint was that there were no safeguards in the agreement as there were in the pact. The Canadian assembly and content rules in the pact safeguarded the Canadian industry. Under the agreement the industry would have to compete. The fact that the Canadian auto industry was competing and operating well above the safeguard levels seemed not to matter at the time. The Free Trade Agreement stood for open competition; the Auto Pact preserved a protected market. Actually, the union's spirited defense of the Auto Pact was in stark contrast to its opposition to it when it was first introduced. However, at that time the union was comparing it to tariff protection, and the union preferred tariff protection to the Auto Pact. What became clear was that it also preferred the Auto Pact to free trade. In other words, the union preferred total protection to partial protection, and partial protection to open competition. Why this love affair with protection?

Most economic analysts in both Canada and the United States see the Free Trade Agreement as positive for jobs in both countries. The expectation is that Canada will benefit most because of the size of the American market—the market to which it gains preferential access. At the same time Canadian firms will have to cope with a difficult adjustment challenge that will, if accomplished successfully, leave the Canadian economy much more efficient. This is where the unions have a problem with the job estimates. From their perspective, increased efficiency means fewer jobs for the same output. They remain unconvinced that increased efficiency will also lead to higher sales. There is no guarantee that it will. The Free Trade Agreement does not hand over U.S. market share to Canada; it merely presents an opportunity for Canadians to seize. So while the result ought to be positive for Canada, there is no guarantee, and that is a problem for many unions. It is probably the uncertainty that troubles the unions most. As it happens, the American unions also came out in opposition to the Free Trade Agreement. This was a curious development since it is highly unlikely that the agreement could lead to lost jobs in both countries, unless one assumes that neither will gain market share at the expense of third countries.

Two things seemed to spark the strong opposition of organized labor to the Free Trade Agreement:

1. Union power is greater the more protected the market. If wage increases and workplace rigidities can be passed on in higher prices, as they can in protected markets, unions will continue to pursue them. If, however, the cost of pursuing them is loss of market share, as it is in open economies, union bargaining power diminishes.

2. Union power is greater the more markets do not change. Rapid transformation away from traditional industries toward knowledge-based activity is not causing job losses in the aggregate, but it may well be causing job losses in those sectors of the economy where unions are strong and growth in those sectors where unions are weak.

Since the Canada-U.S. Free Trade Agreement is likely to accelerate both the move toward an open economy and the speed of response to economic transformation, union opposition was understandable. At the same time, union opposition was not so much based on the welfare of union members as on the welfare of the union as an institution. This is an important distinction. Unions do, in fact, face an institutional crisis from the gradual erosion of their original role in society. Their inability to stem the tide of globalization means of necessity a change in labor-management relations in North America. The change needs to be in the direction of less adversarialism, consistent with the role of unions in countries like Japan that grew up from the outset trying to compete internationally.

Management and labor have to work together, not against one another, if business expects to compete. In Japan it is not just that strikes are rare and of very short duration, it is also that imaginative ideas for improving efficiency and quality regularly flow from the shopfloor. Workers are full partners in productivity improvement. Since the stimulus for most improvements arises on the shopfloor, businesses whose workers are not partners with management are going to have a progressively more difficult time competing with businesses whose workers are.

But how do businesses with an adversarial tradition change to a partnership mode? What changes are needed in North America's labor relations system to shift effectively from protectionism to competition? How do the Japanese do it? To start with, most Japanese unions are company unions rather than industry unions, and workers have lifetime job "security" with their companies. Strikes are infrequent and short because workers identify with their companies and are anxious for them to grow and succeed. Furthermore, management in Japan responds as actively and seriously to a short strike as management in North America does only to a long one. It is impossible, of course, to transplant the Japanese system to North America, where unions and businesses have grown up with a different history. Unions are not usually company-based, and businesses do not offer lifetime contracts. Furthermore, worker loyalty is eroded by frequent takeovers, carve-ups and restructurings in business. Nevertheless, the challenge to compete is not going to disappear. As in golf, we have to play the ball from where it lies: we have to start from where we are. Three suggestions that might help are the following:

1. Union protectionism in the form of compulsory membership and compulsory dues deductions should diminish. Unions should have to compete for the support of workers

through positive programs with which workers identify. In Canada, particularly, business and labor need to face the pressures of the transition from protectionism together.

2. Business managers should be willing to live both with unions and without them. This may mean having employee associations in some plants and unions in others, and letting them compete in terms of productivity and quality. This is not easy to do, but it has the merits of allowing employees a sense of choice and of giving the unions a challenge to compete with. Management's challenge is not to destroy unions but to help them make a constructive transition. As long as large scale buy-outs and restructurings are prevalent, society needs unions.

3. Unions should build a new social mandate for themselves that will win the support of workers. Past battles and achievements, however important, are no longer enough. Most important achievements have been enshrined in law by now anyway, and workers do not see the need for union membership just to perpetuate past gains. At the same time there are important shopfloor challenges that could enhance competitiveness. These have to do with education (literacy), skill training and enhancement and cooperation with management in terms of shopfloor productivity improvements. This kind of change constitutes a major challenge to unions, but one that, if tackled, might win back the support of young workers who have grown increasingly disenchanted about union membership.

Excessive Regulation and Government Intervention

Historians, trying to explain the difference between Canadian and American attitudes toward government, point frequently to the nation-building challenge faced by Canada after early American rejection of a free trade arrangement. It was clearly going to be difficult to build a nation against the flow of economic logic and leave it to a free enterprise system for which economic logic is so important. Government intervention was not just tolerated in Canada, it was welcomed. In fact, the word intervention might well be changed to initiative. Deals and arrangements between business and government to assist in nation building were commonplace. While the United States developed a mistrust of government power, Canada tried to learn how to put government power to use.

However, when a nation is insulated from international competition, it is easy to slip into problems with excessive regulation and costly government initiatives. The record of protected economies achieving sustained productivity leadership is not all that good. Canada, for example, has provided many incentives for regional development, some of which are built into the unemployment insurance scheme. Americans sometimes see these as subsidies to business that create unfair competition and should be subject to countervailing measures. However, business in Canada pays more for unemployment insurance per employee than business in the United States. Business in Canada also pays more for workmen's compensation, but less for medical insurance. When people think narrowly about the idea of a level playing field, they tend to think in terms of harmonization. Canadians are afraid that Americans, under the Free Trade Agreement, will press for harmonization along American lines, and that Canada will be forced to alter its social security programs. The biggest electoral ploy by the opposition was to say that Canada's medicare system was threatened under the Free Trade Agreement. The agreement does not mention social programs at all, but at the same time it does not define what constitutes a subsidy for unfair trade purposes. The negotiators set a five-to-seven-year time period for both sides to come to an agreement on the subsidy question. Opposition politicians were simply exploiting the uncertainty.

What did become clear in Canada was that Canadian social programs were not so much threatened by the agreement itself as by the requirements of international competition. The agreement after all, is based on the national-treatment principle and does not require harmonization. Having to compete, however, may well lead to a gradual reevaluation of government programs and regulations, most of which were established in an era of protection. It is hard to know where this reevaluation will lead.

The Economic Council of Canada, for example, has stated clearly that Canadians are excessively regulated and badly regulated. The fundamental reason in their view is that the national interest is underrepresented in the political process. Well-organized single-interest groups press government relentlessly to act on particular matters. Industry groups often support regulation because it limits competition. As long as the cost of regulation can be passed on to consumers without loss of market share, it will always be easier for governments to regulate than not to regulate. Consumers are not usually organized politically and are seldom aware of the cost of regulation. In these circumstances it is easy for costly duplication and misguided regulation to creep in. Because of such problems the Canadian government has launched an attempt at regulatory reform in which regulatory initiatives are challenged and cost-benefit analyses made public. This kind of regulatory reform will get quite a boost from the Free Trade Agreement.

What has not become all that clear in Canada, and needs to if Canadian businesses are to compete effectively against American businesses, is that Canadians cannot reasonably look to government for leadership. What government has negotiated through the Free Trade Agreement is a competitive environment. It bears repeating that this is not an auto pact with safeguards and guarantees in it. There are no guarantees in free trade, only opportunities. Furthermore, the Free Trade Agreement has reversed the necessity for Canada to build an independent economy in a narrow corridor. The need for government leadership is over. To a significant degree, government can cut back its range of direct incentives to business and can work instead to build a competitive climate. The opportunity to do so comes none too soon. The Canadian government faces an annual deficit in excess of Canadian $30 billion a year—much higher per capita than the U.S. deficit and with a much smaller defense component. About one-third of all Canadian government revenues annually goes to paying interest on the public debt. Canadians have a well-established habit of looking to government for leadership or redress on a wide variety of social issues. At the same time government is faced with having to cut expenditures, which means cutting out or cutting back on existing programs; there is very little fat left. However, in spite of government's growing inability to respond, and in spite of the competition ethic in the Free Trade Agreement, the habit of looking to government for leadership is dying very slowly. The idea that people, businesses, industries and other nongovernmental institutions should tackle problems head-on rather than complain to government about them is too revolutionary. It was always easier in the past to seek government funding first and to look to one's own initiative later. It is not going to be easy for Canadians to withdraw from the government trough, even though the trough is almost empty.

To this point, the major ideological changes under free trade seem to affect Canada more than the United States. Canada, after all, has had the more protected economy over the years and hence inherits a more troublesome legacy in the fruits of that protectionism. To respond to the challenge of international competition, Canada has to reduce internal trade impediments at home, secure the cooperation of labor in industrial restructuring and make sure government regulation does not needlessly impede efficiency. Furthermore, Canadians in general and Canadian business in particular must stop looking to government for economic leadership and take direct entrepreneurial initiative more often. But the United States is not entirely exempt from the need to change. When Canadians hear Americans talking about trade reciprocity, level playing fields and voluntary export restraints, they get worried about what sounds like "born-again" protectionism. Canadians see the Free Trade Agreement as a stepping-stone to freer trade worldwide. What they are afraid of is that too many Americans see it as a stepping-stone to Fortress North America.

THE FORTRESS NORTH AMERICA FEAR

When Europe announced its 1992 initiative, American and Japanese officials expressed their fears by invoking the term

Fortress Europe. The Europeans in turn voiced their fear of Fortress North America resulting from the Canada-U.S. Free Trade Agreement. The fear is not difficult to understand. It is that while lowering internal trade barriers, the trading blocs will build moats around themselves and raise the drawbridges to keep outsiders outside.

The fear is not that North America or Europe will raise tariffs against outside nations. The GATT assures us that this is unlikely to happen. The fear is more subtle. It has to do with nontariff barriers to trade; in particular, nontariff barriers that are not prohibited under the GATT. The trade fears of the 1990s are about voluntary export restraints, level playing fields and reciprocity. Together they constitute a dangerous minefield where fears are exploited with a mixture of truth and guile. Is it possible that the Canada-U.S. Free Trade Agreement, rather than a step toward more open global competition, will become a vehicle to block outsiders? Will protectionism simply move up from a national to a binational preoccupation? It is a danger because both Canada and the United States could benefit from it, at least in the short run. But that is precisely what makes protectionism so beguiling. It does seem so beneficial in the short run, especially when factories are underused and workers are out of jobs. At the same time one of the great global embarrassments of our time is the massive difference in wealth between nations. As globalization shrinks the world, our awareness of the abject and demoralizing poverty of other nations is bound to rise. Many factors, of course, contribute to wealth differentials, including government policies, work habits and education, but to the extent that the absence of opportunity affects all of these, protectionism in rich countries has to bear some of the blame.

What makes protectionism so attractive is that it appears at first glance to help both domestic producers and domestic employment at the same time, especially in times of recession. If we could simply replace foreign goods with domestic goods, we could raise domestic employment levels at the expense of foreigners. Indeed, if we could do this by making domestic goods a better buy for consumers than imported goods, all well and good. It is when we try to do it by blocking consumer access to foreign goods that we harm both ourselves (through higher prices and less selection) and the foreigners (through limiting their markets). In global economic terms, protectionism leads to waste and inefficiency because consumers end up having less choice. Protectionism is a beggar-thy-neighbor policy. It inflicts more pain on others than it achieves gain for oneself. At a time when the global village is shrinking and national interdependence is on the rise, protectionism ought to be thoroughly discredited. Instead it may be changing its stripes and reappearing in a different guise.

Voluntary Export Restraints

During the seventies the United States imposed "voluntary export restraints" on a number of countries exporting steel to the American market. How, one might ask, can a voluntary restraint be imposed? When it is not all that voluntary is the answer. American steel companies claimed that Brazil, Korea, Japan and the EEC were trading steel unfairly. The importers claimed that they were not trading unfairly and that their success in the American market was due to the inefficiency of America's steel producers. From the American perspective, the unfair trade was largely in the form of subsidies that foreign governments gave their steel industries, but the foreign governments, some of which owned their steel industries, claimed that these subsidies were largely for retraining laid-off workers, not for subsidizing exports. As the arguments heated up, and it looked like it was going to be difficult to prove anything either way, the American government suggested that the countries in question agree to limit their exports to the American market to levels consistent with the prior few years. The nations chose to agree. Otherwise it appeared that the United States would place countervailing duties on their steel to offset the subsidies—or the American government's estimate of the subsidies. By "volunteering" to restrain their exports, the other nations automatically gave up the right to protest American actions to the GATT. Canada was exempted from these voluntary export restraints, after vigorous Canadian lobbying, on the grounds that the Canadian steel industry was not an unfair trader.

While aimed primarily at unfair trade, voluntary export restraints work exactly like quotas but without the fear of retaliation by other nations. The economic effect of voluntary export restraints is usually to raise prices. For example, if Japanese car companies faced a limit on the number of cars they could ship into the American market, they would normally ship more of their expensive fully loaded models and would try to raise prices to the point that market demand for their cars was just about at their allowable limit. Domestic producers, in turn, would be inclined to raise their prices also, first, because Japanese prices were higher, and second, because the limit on Japanese imports prevented the Japanese from gaining any further market share. In other words, while Japanese cars would be present in the U.S. market, they would not actually be competing against American cars as long as there was a limit placed on their market share. Remove the limit, and real competition would begin. As long as the limit remains, real market discipline is kept at bay, and consumers lose power to producers.

Voluntary export restraints exist because of weakness in the GATT rules over what constitutes a subsidy. The GATT definition is unclear. The United States takes the position that if nations would agree on a workable set of rules, voluntary export restraints would be unnecessary. Getting the GATT nations to agree is no easy task, however. In fact, the presence of restraints is likely to speed up the process of agreement. In this sense voluntary export restraints can be seen as a positive and temporary step toward a better GATT definition of subsidies. For the most part, in fact, voluntary export restraints are temporary. There is a time limit on them. All too often, however, when they expire they are readily renewed, in spite of their cost in diminished market discipline. While we wait, the protectionism in voluntary export restraints takes its toll.

Furthermore, the nations on the receiving end of export restraints start to use their imaginations too, and this leads to more measures and countermeasures and more intrusion into the affairs of other nations. Europe, for example, has not opened its market to Japanese cars as much as North America has. France and Italy, in particular, have been very protective of their own companies. One result was that Japanese firms began assembling cars in third countries and shipping them from there to Europe. The Europeans claimed that they were still Japanese cars, even if they were made somewhere else. It became a matter of how much local content was in the cars. Then, of course, the Japanese invested in auto production in the United Kingdom on a joint-venture basis, and still Europeans were talking about blocking U.K.-made cars from entering the rest of Europe because they had too much Japanese content. They called these screwdriver plants, nothing more than a place to assemble Japanese components. The next threat Europe will face is likely to be Japanese car exports from the United States and Canada. This will depend, of course, on how exchange rates evolve. But what is clear is that the more interdependent the world becomes, the more difficult it is to take protectionist aim at any one particular country.

Level Playing Fields

The idea of the level playing field is intuitively appealing. It is that foreign competitors should have no unfair advantages over domestic competitors. If a foreign competitor is government-owned and makes a loss or does not have to declare a dividend or gets its capital on preferential terms, it is not competing fairly. The softwood lumber dispute with Canada was fought on these grounds. As mentioned in chapter 2, the dispute was over stumpage fees—the price to cut down trees—which were lower in Canada because of government ownership and management of forest lands. Canadian firms, it was felt, were gaining market share in the United States because they had an unfair advantage. What the United States proposed to do was level the playing field by imposing a countervailing duty on Canadian softwood lumber. Eventually, in a compromise move, Canada agreed to tax exports of softwood lumber so that it could at least keep the revenue. This meant an increase in the price of softwood lumber exports from

Canada to the United States. The expectation was that Canadian softwood lumber would lose market share in the United States to domestic suppliers.

It is not difficult to see that while the level playing field idea invokes visions of fairness and equity, when it is applied, much of the apparent fairness goes out the window. It has the potential to become extremely intrusive into other countries' affairs. Too often a level playing field comes to mean our playing field or the playing field of whoever imposes it. Underlying it is the view that foreigners could not possibly be succeeding in North American markets without cheating in some way or another. Take the unfair element out of trade, and the American trade deficit would be reversed at once. This perspective is much easier on the ego than having to acknowledge the superiority of some foreign competitors and the need to learn from them. Under the level playing field concept it is they who must change their ways. Furthermore, there seems to be no limit to the scope of the level playing field concept. Countervailing duties end up getting applied to more and more circumstances, all in the name of fairness.

Reciprocity

Another form of unfair trade occurs when countries limit imports into their own market while busily exporting into everyone else's. Japan is the prime example. For a long time Japan blocked access to its market not by conventional tariff and nontariff barriers but by cultural factors that limited outsider access to distribution channels and government contracts. Japanese consumers developed strong preferences for Japanese goods. Foreign cars, appliances, cameras and television sets were a rarity in Japan. Japanese attitudes about imports are changing and the obstacles are coming down, but very slowly. Japan initially took the view that Japanese consumer preferences were based rationally on the superiority of Japanese goods. Other nations were unconvinced as long as Japanese consumers had little real choice. Japan then claimed that the real problem was that too few North Americans and Europeans spoke the Japanese language and understood Japanese customs, and that while they had embarked on extensive language training themselves, North America had not. This complaint is harder to refute.

The problem arising from these concerns is that countries facing large trade deficits with Japan have begun to argue for reciprocity. They want to introduce rules that would deny market access to countries whose own markets are not open. Again, this seems fair on the surface. Why should we allow foreigners into our markets if they will not allow us into theirs? It is a reasonable question. But when one tries to apply the idea in practice, it can have perverse effects because reciprocity is usually measured not by opportunity but by results. The test of whether a given foreign market is open has become not so much a set of rules as a measurement of sales. If American cars or televisions are not selling reasonably in Japan, it is because Japan's market is not open. All too quickly, reciprocity gets used to blunt market discipline. The danger in reciprocity from this perspective is that instead of trying to improve their products so that they genuinely compete, European and North American firms will try to force the Japanese to accept them the way they are or face exclusion from European and American markets. Market discipline is blunted, and consumers suffer. There is, on the other hand, much legitimacy in reciprocity when its thrust is to open up the markets of Japan and other key exporter nations so that consumers there face a genuine choice between local and imported goods.

Level playing fields, voluntary restraints and reciprocity have a nice ring to them. They are terms chosen carefully to avoid any semblance of protectionism. The emphasis is on fairness. Who can be opposed to that? In their implementation, however, the emphasis tends to shift from establishing fair rules to getting desired results. The process is often called managed trade. This is an appropriate term. It implies that trade should not be left to the vagaries of a competitive market but should be managed and made more predictable. Managed by whom? By governments, it would seem. Many people might be opposed to that. The major benefits of international trade are efficiency and consumer choice. Managed trade in the form of level playing fields, reciprocity and voluntary restraints threatens both by weakening market discipline and does this innocuously with the best of intentions, as it were.

The Fortress Europe and Fortress North America concerns of the 1990s are bound up not so much with tariffs and quotas as with the subtleties of managed trade. Reducing the efficiency and discipline of the domestic market by government intervention is not a concept that would win much grass roots support in the United States. Doing the same thing in the international market seems to be a different matter. Managed trade has support in both Europe and the United States, in part because it is presented as fairness at home—its teeth are bared only in the implementation phase—and because it is aimed at Japan and reassures us that Japan's success is due more to unfair trade than to competitive superiority. Managed trade assuages our egos. It is not, however, good business. When one nation or region begins to dictate to others the terms of access to its market, power is shifted from producing nations to consuming nations, and the global market rewards to greater efficiency are thereby blunted.

But if managed trade is an inefficient instrument, how then should we deal with unfair trade issues like export subsidies and closed markets? What is the alternative to Fortress Europe and Fortress North America? It is the use of multilateral institutions such as the GATT and shared rule setting with other nations. In other words, instead of one nation or trading bloc imposing on others its definition of reciprocity or a level playing field, the definitions should be worked out jointly with input from all nations affected. But is this not a slow and cumbersome procedure? It certainly has been in the past. If we want to prevent more global "fortresses," however, we need to find ways of making multilateral institutions work better. The main thrust of both Europe 1992 and the Canada-U.S. Free Trade Agreement is to remove traditional trade impediments. Fortress building is not their primary goal. But the fortress fear is real because of the subtle nature of the new protectionism and the tendency of both Europe and the United States to frame their own rules and impose them on others. Globalization is supposed to be moving us toward a greater sense of interdependence between nations, a sense that the international implications of domestic policy matter. We ought to be strengthening international arrangements that promote interdependence, rather than having one nation impose its will on the others. Hopefully, the binational panel will prove to be such an arrangement between Canada and the United States. The rule of law in the long run always works better than bullying by the strong. Beyond that, North America should redouble its efforts to work within the GATT toward acceptable and better-defined trade legislation. Canada should be especially active. When a nation is small in economic power, workable rules are more important. Cooperation and inter-dependence are part of the ideology of free trade.

A LEAP OF FAITH

Donald Macdonald, a prominent Canadian statesman and ex-politician, became a convert to free trade as a result of heading a royal commission on Canada-U.S. relations (The Royal Commission on the Economic Union and Development Prospects for Canada). In recommending that Canada open negotiations with the United States on free trade, Macdonald described this as a leap of faith for Canada. The description was greeted with derision by his opponents and embarrassment by his supporters. Leaps of faith are not in vogue in Canada. Analysts promptly attempted to measure the likely impact of a free trade agreement more precisely, but found themselves unable to do it with any consensus. How many new jobs would it create? In which industries? In Canada or in the United States? How would it affect direct investment, consumer prices and aggregate productivity? Precise answers were not forth-coming. Reassurances were. So were disagreements. The more the dialogue went on in Canada, the more it seemed that Canadians were going to have to take a leap of faith.

Dealing with Complex Issues in a Democracy

One of the difficulties with Canada's election dialogue will be familiar to Americans. The difficulty was a political one. Simply put, it was how to deal with complex issues in a democratic election. Free trade was a complex issue and an important one at that. Why not have the issue debated by leading politicians and analysts and let people come to whatever judgment they would? As Americans learned in their general election, political debates are often short on substance. This is not entirely because politicians are short on substance, but because their "handlers" and "managers" are more concerned about the possibility of a political mistake being made during the heat of debate. They presumably think that this is a more likely occurrence than a brilliant impromptu remark that they themselves did not formulate. For whatever reason, American politicians ended up debating through prepared statements that lacked any of the dynamism of a real exchange of views, while Canadian politicians did have genuine debates but managed to see to it that they lacked substance.

The most common plea of Canadian voters was for more substantive information about the specific terms of the Free Trade Agreement and how it compared to the Common Market in Europe. What they got instead was a "trust me" message from the party in power and a range of scare tactics from the opposition parties. The scare tactics focussed mainly on the loss of sovereignty and identity in Canada and the threat to Canada's universal health-care system. Opposition politicians and their advisors knew full well that under the national-treatment principle sovereignty was not really threatened, and with separate currencies neither was the health-care system, but they gambled that the public would not know. They also knew that closer economic integration alone did not necessarily mean loss of sovereignty. Canada and the United States have been growing closer economically for the last twenty years, and these have been years when Canada has introduced many unique social initiatives. It is difficult to escape the view that integrity and the public good are not always the first instincts of those in pursuit of political power. One of the low points of the Canadian campaign was the nationwide circulation of a newspaper supplement titled "What's the Big Deal?"—a sort of cartoon parody of Mulroney, Reagan and Uncle Sam. Stridently anti-American in tone, it presented a very biased set of answers to key questions and took particular delight in making fun of Macdonald's "leap of faith." Its impact was undoubtedly enhanced by the governing party's decision to try to persuade rather than educate the Canadian public.

At one stage a retired provincial court judge from Alberta, Marjorie Bowker, examined the Free Trade Agreement herself and wrote a book about it. She became something of a cause célèbre in Canada. As it happened, she was opposed to free trade, and her arguments did not win the day. She became a cause célèbre because she tried to inject some real substance into what had become a superficial debate of entrenched institutions. How should developed democratic societies deal with complex issues? Is it really necessary for politicians to assume a "soap-opera" mentality on the part of voters? Are they just being realistic? Are complex issues simply beyond the public's understanding? To the extent that they are, democracies are in a fragile state. If we are heading into a period of greater interdependence between nations, we are also heading toward increasingly complex issues. The need for broader public understanding of other cultures and countries is greater than the North American media in general are prone to show. European students on exchange programs in North American universities frequently express feelings of being cut off from the rest of the world. The information flows about world affairs that they are used to are simply not available here.

Democratic societies require an educated, informed and curious public to handle complex issues effectively. Media hype, scare tactics and "trust me" approaches are much more dangerous to the freedoms democracies enshrine. Education must improve, and so must public media coverage of international affairs. Otherwise Canadians and Americans will end up taking leaps of faith when it is not necessary to leap—when with a little effort information could have been obtained to make the choice more rationally.

The Limits of Rationality

Some decisions, however, cannot be made through analysis because their effects cannot be entirely foreseen. The Free Trade

Agreement falls into this category. It is difficult to justify free trade scientifically or from observation. Before the fact, it is difficult to know how free trade will work out because its benefits come in the form of an opportunity rather than a sure thing. After the fact, it is difficult to separate the effects of free trade from the effects of other economic and social developments. When the results are finally available, they will be too mushy to make a judgment. Consequently, the decision to shift toward freer trade and greater interdependence has to be made largely on faith in general economic principles that have worked for us in the past. This is particularly troublesome to societies that have largely abandoned faith and tradition in favor of rationality, enlightenment and reason, because many economic principles are more the product of tradition than reason. Take, for example, the efficacy of market discipline. No individual facing tough competition likes it. Most, reasonably enough, try to avoid it. But when societies as a whole try to avoid it, their economic performance and often their basic freedoms suffer. The principle of market discipline has become a tradition because it works, not because people find it appealing in practice.

In his insightful book, *The Fatal Conceit*,[1] F. A. Hayek describes the scientific "spirit of the age" as one rooted in the primacy of reason and evidence. He sees socialist thought, in particular, as dominated by the view that society should not pursue a given course unless its purpose is fully understood and specified in advance and unless its effects can be shown to be positive. In general, socialists in Canada opposed free trade. It was an issue that rose above the confines of rational socialist thought. But the nonsocialists had a hard time defending it. After all, nobody wanted to appear irrational in public. Having to resort to tradition and leaps of faith was awkward. But as Hayek points out, reason did not create tradition, but tradition has certainly inspired economic performance. For Canadians, free trade was an ideological leap of faith, not an incremental step down a cautious, rational, well-trodden path. Canadians debated it and eventually took it. Having done so, Canadians would find it easier to deal with global Americans rather than protectionist Americans.

CONCLUSION

There is an ideological side to free trade that brings out passionate feelings in those committed to the positivistic rationality of socialism. The arguments in support of protectionism are much easier to make in rational terms, using the evidence of import levels industry by industry. The arguments in support of free trade are more general and more related to a belief in the efficacy of competition and freedom over central control and regulation. This chapter has suggested that protectionism leaves a legacy of internal strife in the form of balkanization, adversarial labor relations and excessive government intervention and regulation. For Canada, the conversion to free trade requires an ideological change that will result in dismantling internal trade barriers, transforming labor relations and freeing enterprise. Americans may well view such changes as very desirable for Canada, but otherwise of no great concern to them. The risk of Fortress North America makes them of concern, however. If outsider nations are progressively stripped of their competitive edge through managed trade, Canada and the United States will become more and more dependent on one another, and this will not be healthy for Canada. The arguments for Fortress North America are similar to the arguments for protectionism. They are rational and can be supported with concrete evidence. Furthermore, Canada's experience with balkanization as one of the fruits of protectionism leaves Canadians uneasy about the potential damage to Canada-U.S. free trade of a Fortress North America outcome.

Canada ended up having to take a leap of faith in regard to free trade. The United States may need to take a similar leap in regard to its own protectionist instincts. Competition and the rule of law have long served as important traditions in nations with the greatest freedom and progress. They need very much to be applied to our international affairs. One of the reasons so many nations around the world are beginning to examine new approaches to economic growth and progress is that Japan has shown that it is possible with the right policies and circumstances to rise to the top in world trade. Japan has done it by competing. The market really is free. There is hope for others. It would be a shame to spoil it now by building trade fortresses and blocking the progress of those who would follow suit. The world will be richer if instead we encourage them and have recourse to the rule of law to ensure fairness. Free trade must not stop at the borders of North America.

NOTE

1. F. A. Hayek, *The Fatal Conceit* (Chicago: University of Chicago Press, 1988), pp. 60–62.

4

THE GLOBALIZATION OF
COMPETITION

It is time now to come down to earth from the rarefied heights of ideology to the practicalities of global competition. After all, North America has lived quite contentedly for decades with protectionist inefficiencies built into the economy, Canada more so than the United States. Were it not for Japan, the pressure to change would be quite muted, however well justified. However, when Japanese firms began to take an increasing share of North American markets, people started to pay attention. Sometimes, of course, the attention focussed on what the Japanese were doing wrong: unfair trade practices and restricted access to their market. In this chapter we focus more on what they do right: product quality, global strategy and rapid innovation. There is something innately quixotic about Americans, who in a free market choose to buy so many Japanese goods and at the same time chide the Japanese for not buying more American goods. Other Americans, to their credit, are facing the Japanese challenge head-on. They are interested in competing more effectively. Organizing the firm to compete more effectively in the global market is the subject of this chapter. In the next chapter we look at the implications of globalization on parent-subsidiary relations. Can Canadian subsidiaries, under the Free Trade Agreement, play a significant role in their parents' quest for global competitiveness? If so, how might that role be defined? But we turn first to the challenge facing parent companies who, unlike Zenith, which tried to fight the color-television battle by blocking the Japanese, intend to do battle head-on through product improvements and through global strategies and structures.

ELEMENTAL FORCES SHAPING GLOBALIZATION

Who would have believed ten years ago that *glasnost* and *perestroika* would shake the Soviet economic system to its core? Non-Communist governments in Poland and Hungary would have seemed like a wild-eyed dream. It certainly would have seemed improbable that China should have abandoned its doctrinaire Maoism in favor of economic growth. Maybe it still is improbable. That Europe should have set aside its ageless internal squabbles and committed itself to building a genuine common market by 1992 is quite extraordinary. That Canada and the United States should have signed a Free Trade Agreement after 120 years of trying is equally remarkable. But that all of these should have occurred in the same decade borders on the incredible and craves an explanation.

At the heart of the explanation is Japan. As figure 4.1 shows, the overall effect of these momentous events has been to make the world smaller and more accessible and to make possible a global approach to business. What Japan did was to seize the opportunities first. In so doing, the Japanese demonstrated that it is possible with effort and technology to rise to the top in the world of business. They outperformed Europe and North America, and in doing so they sent a message to the rest of the world that the market really is free. Upstarts can rise to the top. The four tigers of Asia—Hong Kong, Singapore, South Korea and Taiwan—are busy developing their versions of the Japanese strategy.

Figure 4.1
Elemental Forces Shaping Globalization

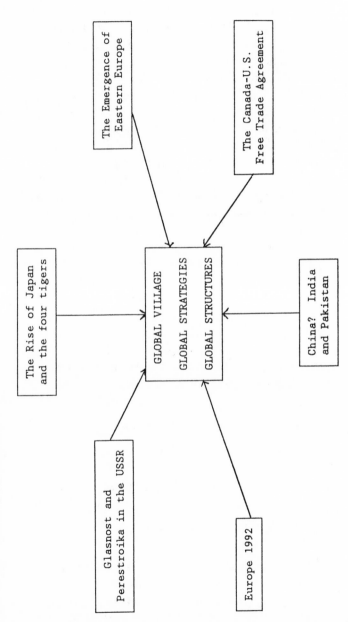

From this perspective, Europe had to get its house in order because of the challenge from Japan. So did Canada and the United States. Europe 1992 takes direct aim at wasteful regulations that hinder efficiency. The Canada-U.S. Free Trade Agreement permits a more efficient restructuring of North American industry. It was the Japanese challenge that forced the pace of both by increasing the cost of delaying change. Before the Japanese challenge, the cost of inefficiency was higher consumer prices; after, it was loss of market share, and that is a much higher cost. As Europe and North America took steps to increase their efficiency, it seemed that the world was poised for a massive move forward in wealth and technology. The fear in Eastern Europe was of being left irrevocably behind. An interesting feature of these unparalleled developments was that politicians, in general, were in the caboose rather than leading the way. To be sure, the Canada-U.S. Free Trade Agreement and Europe 1992 have required political commitment, but the reality is that the desire for change among the people had got ahead of the politicians. This is not surprising. Politicians are too often consumed by domestic affairs, and the challenge was coming from abroad. Furthermore, the globalization of economic activity diminishes the relevance of nation-state boundaries and with it the importance of national governments in economic affairs. Technology, not politics, has been leading the way.

WHAT IS A GLOBAL STRATEGY?

The concept of a global strategy contains the following elements:

1. Products are designed from the outset for the requirements of major world markets.

2. Production takes place in large-scale, modern, specialized facilities.

3. Quality, efficiency and flexibility are achieved through technically advanced, computer-directed manufacturing.

4. Products are launched in all major world markets quickly.

5. Advertising and promotion programs emphasize global similarities.
6. Control is achieved through use of a global management information system.

At first glance, the elements of a global strategy display a clear disregard for national boundaries and a preference for intelligent centralization of strategic activity. The word intelligent is important. Effective globalization strategies have to be much more informed about global market conditions than is implied by the old "do it our way" approach from the head office. Nevertheless, there seems to be little room for independent subsidiaries in a global strategy. Compliance with central control is at the heart of it. Global strategies have much more in common with integration and single markets than with independence and national differences.

DO GLOBAL STRATEGIES ALWAYS WORK?

Business executives see a number of pressures in the international environment pushing them toward a global rather than a nation-state perspective in their strategic thinking. These have been mentioned in earlier chapters, but it is useful to repeat them at this point.

1. Declining tariffs and the emergence of regional trading blocs are facilitating world trade.
2. Global telecommunications, particularly satellite television transmissions, are leading to common consumer tastes throughout major markets of the world.
3. Computer and fax technologies are making global coordination easier.
4. Shipping costs have been reduced and transit times cut.
5. The Japanese have succeeded in international markets by effectively implementing global strategies.

One of the consequences of these pressures is that world trade has increased rapidly as barriers inhibiting it have been removed. From 1984 to 1988 net world exports climbed 51 percent to the annual level of U.S. $2.7 trillion. The increase was a staggering 36 percent from 1986 to 1988 alone. By comparison, foreign direct investment flows for this same period averaged well under U.S. $50 billion, with only modest increases in the volume of investment flows evident. The growth of world exports has also outstripped the growth of world GDP, especially in the seventies and eighties, and especially from the leading industrial countries where the barriers have been lowered the most. Trade once again is challenging foreign investment for dominance in the global economy.

At the same time there are pressures toward localization that are mitigating globalization strategies, especially in certain countries. The following are some of the leading pressures:

1. World trade is still hindered by escalating nontariff barriers and new forms of protectionism.

2. Foreign-exchange problems keep many nations out in the cold, especially the nations of Africa, South America, Eastern Europe, the Soviet Union and China.

3. Cultural differences lead to unique consumer preferences. Tradition and religion make people different. World products may miss the mark.

4. New production technology is reducing the benefits of large-scale production and making possible the customizing of products to markets at a more reasonable cost.

These pressures suggest that it can be dangerous to think only in terms of "world products" and global marketing strategies. At the same time global strategies have worked in some industries with some products. For some industries, international trade accounts for a greater share of output than for other more domestic industries. These are the global industries where competition is truly international. A camera or a stereo, for example, seldom has

Figure 4.2
Locating Industries on a Globalization-Localization Matrix

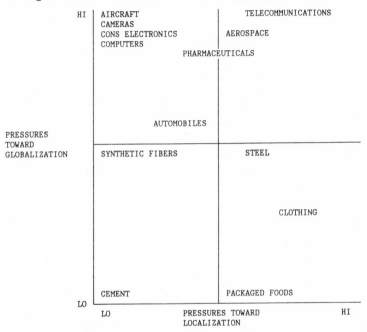

Sources: See Figure 4.3.

to be localized to sell in different markets. Packaged foods, on the other hand, and some shoes and clothing can be greatly influenced by local tastes and traditions. Figure 4.2 shows how some industries fit on a globalization-localization matrix. It is a very presumptive figure—for example, high-fashion clothing is much more global than ordinary clothing—but it is still useful in that it forces us to look at the effect of globalization on different industries and raises the specter that global strategies do not always work.

LOCATING AN INDUSTRY ON THE MATRIX

Finding the right quadrant for a given industry entails asking two basic questions:

1. How important are scale efficiencies in either production, marketing or research and development (R & D)?
2. How much local adaptation is needed for different markets?

In the two right quadrants of the figure, local adaptation is seen to be important. In the two top quadrants, scale efficiencies of some kind are seen to be important. The top left quadrant is where local differences are minor and the benefits of globalization significant. For example, the demand for cameras is thought to be quite similar from market to market; the same features are valued similarly by Swedish, British, Japanese or American users. At the same time, there are high design and engineering costs in cameras, and production is usually automated and scale-sensitive. In this sense cameras are good global products, as are aircraft, computers and consumer electronics. The bottom right quadrant is where local differences matter and the benefits of globalization are not so significant. The examples this time are clothing and packaged foods, where local tastes and preferences really do make a difference. It takes an intimate familiarity with a given industry to place it appropriately. There are always competitive segments within industries that defy the kind of generalization that the matrix tries to impose. There are also industries where both scale efficiencies and local adaptation are important. One example, in the top right quadrant, is telecommunications, an industry utilizing expensive and rapidly evolving technology and yet also facing national markets with quite different systems already in place.

GLOBALIZATION AND CORPORATE STRUCTURE

It is now time to impose on the matrix the kind of corporate structure appropriate for the various quadrants (see figure 4.3). The global structure in the top left quadrant is a type of corporate structure that emphasizes central control. The multinational structure in the two lower quadrants emphasizes, in contrast, strong local

Figure 4.3
Organizational Consequences of Internationalization

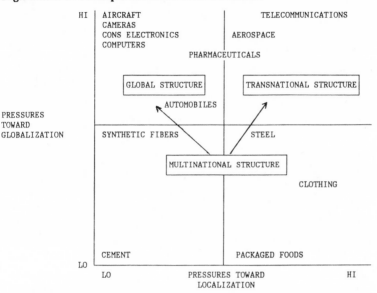

Sources: Figures 4.2 and 4.3 are based on three related papers: Gunnar Hedlund, "The Hypermodern MNC—A Heterarchy?" *Human Resource Management* 25, no. 1 (Spring 1986): 9–31; Christopher A. Bartlett and Sumantra Ghoshal, "Organizing for Worldwide Effectiveness: The Transnational Solution," *California Management Review*, Fall 1988, 54–74; and, Herbert Henzler and Wilhelm Rall, "Facing up to the Globalization Challenge," *McKinsey Quarterly*, Fall 1986, 52–68.

autonomy. The transnational structure in the top right quadrant tries for both a global efficiency and local responsiveness. More information about these three types of structure is given later in the chapter.

The impression given in figure 4.3 is that consumer electronics firms that operate internationally will do so through a global organization structure, and clothing firms through a multinational organization structure. The real world, however, is seldom so tidy. How firms ought to organize and how they do in practice can be quite different. Christoher A. Bartlett and Sumantra Ghoshal in their recent book *Managing across Borders*[1] pointed out two interesting illustrations. One had to do with the consumer electronics industry—top left quadrant—where Matsushita with its global approach had taken a significant market share from Philips in Europe. One key reason was that Philips was organized as a multinational with strong country managers and could not achieve global efficiencies in design and production because central control was lacking. The other example had to do with the consumer packaged goods industry—bottom right quadrant—where Japanese competitor Kao, despite high product quality and efficiency, was unable to take market share from Procter and Gamble and Unilever, because the latter had strong country managers and Kao did not. This sounds contradictory. The point was that strong local managers were an asset in the consumer packaged goods industry because significant local adaptation was necessary. The product had to be packaged and marketed to distinctive local tastes. Kao called the shots centrally, and this did not work. These examples illustrate that corporate structure can get in the way of performance if it is not correctly aligned with the competitive realities of the industry. In an industry where scale efficiencies are significant and local adaptation is not, use a global structure. In an industry where local adaptation matters and scale efficiencies are not significant, use a multinational structure. When both are significant, use a transnational approach—a kind of in-between way of trying to have it all.

In general, Japanese firms have had a tendency to use a global approach to international markets. European firms have used a multinational approach more frequently—perhaps an aftermath of colonialism. American firms seem to have come out in between but have used the multinational approach more when tariffs were high and markets were insulated from trade. For America and Europe, responding to the Japanese challenge really means shifting the culture of their firms from a multinational to a more global approach. Among the developed nations of the world, in particular, tariffs genuinely have dropped and consumer tastes genuinely have coalesced. This cannot be said of the less developed countries of the world, and that is a serious problem, but from a business standpoint the big opportunity under globalization is in the developed nations. For the present, that is where the profits are. The surge in Japanese foreign investment occurred during the eighties when the pressures toward globalization were already clear. American and European firms invested abroad in a different era and now face the need to change their historic way of doing things.

CONTRASTING GLOBAL AND MULTINATIONAL APPROACHES

Global corporations conceive and design products for world markets from the outset. Frequently, subsidiaries in key markets have input into product design, but once the parent organization launches a new product, the subsidiary's role reverts to that of implementer. Global products are usually marketed to international similarities rather than to cultural differences, and marketing strategies are therefore established as a rule in the parent organization. Products are manufactured wherever in the world the necessary quality standards can be achieved at the lowest cost, including transportation to key markets. As a practical matter, large markets attract production because market share is often enhanced by the presence of a production facility. Also, host-country governments sometimes induce local production through nontariff barriers to trade, but the classic global strategy is conceived without such artificial impediments to the movement of goods.

Under such a strategy corporate subsidiaries around the world cannot operate with a great deal of autonomy. They become an integrated part of a global organization and often play no strategic role at all. If production does take place in a particular subsidiary, it will often be specialized production of a single model or component for use throughout the corporation. Hence the design and specification of what is produced is seldom handled by the subsidiary because it is not aimed primarily at the subsidiary's market. In these conditions coordination between parent and subsidiaries is critical and is often achieved by sending parent executives to run subsidiary operations for two-to-three-year terms. Specialization is at the heart of global company strategies. Subsidiaries are primarily obedient and are evaluated as cost centers. The profit-center concept just does not fit the strategy. Global subsidiaries have little strategic autonomy and take few if any initiatives.

Multinational corporations, by way of contrast, develop products for their own market or region and then offer them for sale or adaptation by their overseas subsidiaries. Subsidiaries have the capacity to absorb parent-company technology and adapt the resulting products to local conditions and tastes. In many multinational subsidiaries that technological capacity grows over time into full-fledged R & D capable of independent product innovation. Traditionally, multinational subsidiaries manufacture products for their own national markets, adapting the parent-company product line as required. If specialization is at the heart of global strategies, duplication and autonomy are at the heart of multinational strategies. "One word from the head office and we do as we please" is the rule at the extreme. In the pure multinational model it is technology and skills that cross national boundaries, not products. It is a model born in an era of high tariff protection.

Under a multinational strategy the subsidiary or country manager has a higher level of autonomy because the emphasis is on adaptation to local conditions. Multinational subsidiaries are organized by region and country rather than by product line and are evaluated by profit-center criteria keyed to results rather than obedience. Usually, local nationals are appointed as country managers, and turnover is relatively slow. Each subsidiary takes on a character and personaltiy of its own and formulates its own internal strategy. The role of country manager and region manager is similar to the role of the parent chief executive officer (CEO), except for the more limited geographical sphere of activity. To establish the contrast more clearly, table 4.1 summarizes the essential differences between global and multinational organizations.

The biggest weaknesses in the global model are the growing dependence of the subsidiaries on the parent over time and the lack of substantive ideas or initiatives arising in the subsidiaries. The biggest weakness in the multinational model is the difficulty the

Table 4.1
Contrasting Global and Multinational Structures

	Global Structure	Multinational Structure
product line	specialized	duplicated
market emphasis	international	national
transfers	product	technology and skills
evaluation mode	cost center	profit center
subsidiary role	implement strategy	develop and implement strategy
subsidiary autonomy	low	high
subsidiary management	foreign, short-term	local, long-term

parent has in imposing an overarching strategy on its autonomous subsidiaries and hence obtaining some of the benefits of specialization. These weaknesses are enhanced when a company adopts a strategy inconsistent with its product-market thrust. In other words, if a company needs a lot of subsidiary input about local markets because national differences are important to how the product is designed and sold, and it adopts a global structure, then lack of subsidiary initiative becomes a serious impediment. On the other hand, if a company can greatly increase its efficiency by rearranging its production and standardizing needless differences but has adopted a multinational structure, then the autonomy of subsidiary managers becomes a serious impediment.

THE TRANSNATIONAL OPTION

We turn next to the top right quadrant of figure 4.3. What should be clear by now is that there are serious potential problems with both the global and multinational structures. One gets you greater efficiencies and the other gets you greater local responsiveness. Since there is really no such thing as a perfect organization anyway, one is tempted to suggest simply picking the one closest to the company's product-market thrust and learning to live with the organizational deficiencies. For many firms that is sound advice. There are, however, a number of firms for whom either deficiency is too costly. Telecommunications is a good illustration. There are powerful pressures toward globalization from high R & D costs and available scale economies, and also powerful pressures toward localization from differences in the systems in place in each country and in the politicization of the industry. Firms facing such challenges sometimes try to capture the benefits of both the global and the multinational structures. So, incidentally, do firms who have some product divisions that suit the global structure and other product divisions better suited to the multinational structure.

Theoretically the transnational structure achieves the optimal blend of global efficiency and local responsiveness. Subsidiary managers have autonomy but act within the parameters of overall corporate strategy. Subsidiary managers have local market knowledge but also a knowledge of international markets. But these descriptive statements do not constitute a definition of the transnational structure. How does a firm know when it has one? For some, the presence of a shared-responsibility matrix structure is the best evidence. In such a structure geographic areas and product divisions share responsibility for subsidiary decisions. The idea is that by sharing the responsibility one forces a constructive dialogue through which the best decision emerges. In this sense the best decision is one that balances the need for local adaptation with the need for global efficiency. Since the optimal balance is subjective and constantly shifting, it is difficult for a firm to know whether it has achieved it regardless of the structure it follows. Furthermore, people's egos sometimes get in the way, and the matrix structure often fails to achieve its purpose. It is entirely possible to have a transnational perspective without a matrix structure. One simply finds a way to put the matrix mentality into the heads of country managers or of product division managers, as the case may be.

If the transnational perspective is so elusive, how can a firm know whether it has achieved it? There are some distinguishing characteristics, and it is useful to establish what they are.

1. Subsidiaries in transnational organizations have strong local boards of directors with both head-office and local

representation. These boards hammer out key strategic decisions. Often local boards include strong individuals who are outsiders to the firm. Du Pont operates its Canadian subsidiary this way, as do GE, Union Carbide and many others.

2. Subsidiary managers are active at multiple levels on the key operating and project committees of the parent. There are frequent opportunities for learning and influencing for both the parent and the subsidiary.

3. Subsidiary managers have global opportunities with certain of the products they produce. These are normally earned by subsidiary initiative in R & D or through subsidiary acquisitions. Global product mandates require the subsidiary CEO to be active on the senior policy committees of the parent.

4. Subsidiary managers are actively in contact with the managers of key corporate subsidiaries in other countries. They may be looking to buy from them, sell to them, learn from them or teach them.

5. The company has built up a strong corporate culture and a shared vision of its overall style and mission. At the same time subsidiary managers are allowed considerable freedom to implement the vision in their own countries.

What is clear from these characteristics is that they are more about managerial attitude than about organizational structure. In this sense the transnational is more an ideal than a structure. However, what it stands for is important to companies anxious to keep good people in their subsidiaries throughout the world. Without good people, it is difficult for an organization to learn about critical commercial information elsewhere in the world. Without an interesting role or mandate for the subsidiary, it is difficult to hold on to good talent there, and the company grows increasingly dependent on head-office talent. When this occurs, the ability of the company to learn and adapt is impaired. In industries with rapidly evolving technology or rapid style changes, impaired learning can be dangerous. The transnational approach is really about learning. It is about raising the awareness level of key executives worldwide about the corporate mission and providing them an ongoing opportunity to influence it. It is much more about style, attitude and mind-set than it is about formal organizational structure.

THE TRANSITION TO A GLOBAL STRUCTURE

Given the preponderance of globalization pressures in the economic environment, the traditional multinational subsidiary with its high autonomy and domestic focus is not likely to endure unscathed. Increasingly, international companies are going to abandon the multinational structure in favor of either the global or the transnational structure. The transition is not likely to be without pain. Moving to a global structure means imposing corporate will on hitherto autonomous subsidiaries. It means changing subsidiary mandates and reducing strategic independence. There are going to be many subsidiary wrecks on the shoals of globalization. Some of the steps parents must consider in the transition to a global structure are as follows:

Determine Where the Critical Scale Economies and Other Benefits of Globalization Lie

Offshore production is often the first thought of North American firms threatened by import competition. Put the labor-intensive production processes into a low-wage country and otherwise continue business as usual. A globalization strategy, however, implies much more than this. Products need to be designed for key world markets, and design needs to be sensitive to production processes and to global standards of product reliability. Under globalization the issue is not where we can make it cheaper, but where we can achieve the best combination of technology, quality and cost. On this basis, different products end up being manufactured in different countries. Some factories concentrate on component parts. But each factory is set up to serve the corporation's worldwide needs, or at least a major portion of them. Many large corporations are nervous about having single sources of supply of key products or components. The cost of a strike or other disruption can be enormous. They therefore often develop two or three sources, but they normally designate one factory as the prime source and assign to it the ongoing related product-development responsibility. Other competing units within the corporation may over time try to displace it as the prime source based on superior cost-quality performance. Competition within the firm can be as healthy as competition in the market. This is certainly how Du Pont views the world.

While production scale economies are an important benefit of globalization, they are not the only benefit. Advertising and promotion can be global too. It is just as possible to advertise to global similarities as to national differences, but to do this successfully requires a high level of understanding of the mood and mind-set of different regions. There is an enormous difference between successful global advertising and the view that what is good for Iowa or Texas is good for the rest of the world. The same is true for global design.

The benefits of globalization will not be the same for all products or industries. It is useful to establish where they are greatest. How homogeneous are customer needs from one country to another? What savings are possible from designing the product for global markets and manufacturing it to global capacity? What technology does large-scale specialized production make possible? What problem might arise in particular countries or regions from such an approach? As questions like these are answered product line by product line, it is possible to identify where globalization fits best and where localization is more important.

Establish a Role or Mandate for Each Major Subsidiary: Which Products Does It Produce for Which Markets?

Most major subsidiaries end up with mixed mandates according to the depth of technological and managerial skill in the subsidiary.

Once an analysis is done of the globalization potential of the various products the corporation is involved with, the subsidiary may be assigned a global role with some products and a local role with others. In other words, it may continue as a multinational subsidiary for products with important local differences and function as a global subsidiary for global products. This makes the subsidiary hard to manage but makes eminent sense strategically for the corporation. The subsidiary ends up producing some items for the local or regional market only, importing some from other subsidiaries and producing some for world markets. It is useful therefore to make the subsidiary's mandate clear to avoid confusion within the corporation as a whole.

Reduce the Strategic Autonomy of Subsidiaries

Globalization means imposing corporate will on country managers who, under the multinational structure, were quite autonomous. This imposition of corporate will may take the form of ordering cessation of subsidiary production of certain products in favor of globally designed products made in other subsidiaries. Or it may mean redesign of a subsidiary's product to global specifications and production of it in the subsidiary for world markets in a new, very modern facility. In either case the "not invented here" syndrome may intervene, or simply the natural resistance to change. Under globalization, the subsidiary manager's power has to be constrained and brought into harmony with global corporate thinking. Country managers with international skills can make such a transition; others cannot and have to go.

Try to Retain the Critical Strengths of the Subsidiary through the Kind of Mandate Assigned

Some multinational subsidiaries are huge organizations with thousands of employees and a long history, tradition and culture of their own. Furthermore, they have significant technological and managerial depth and are frequently tapped by the head office for key

eople in the globalization strategy. There is no reason to suppose
hat successful global executives are more likely to be found in the
ead office than in the subsidiaries, especially if the subsidiaries
have had a long history of autonomy. This brings us to a dilemma.
Subsidiaries without strategic autonomy have trouble attracting
and keeping good people. Corporations embarking on global
strategies need good people with a knowledge of world markets.

The kind of mandate assigned to a subsidiary will influence the
kind of people who will work there in the long term, and that in
turn will influence the kind of mandate possible in the future. If a
subsidiary has built up significant technological or managerial
expertise over the years and is assigned a mandate that emphasizes
its role as a production site only, its accumulated expertise will
soon be gone. From this perspective, subsidiaries are just as
interested in obtaining a product-design role, a marketing role, an
R & D role and other professional functions as they are in obtaining
a world production role.

Rotate Country Managers More Frequently to Help Them Develop a Global Vision

Country managers with long-term local appointments do not
easily develop global perspectives, and it is difficult to globalize
an organization successfully without those perspectives in place.
One way to accelerate globalization is to move senior people from
one international subsidiary to another or from subsidiary to head
office and back. Of course, this means sending in nonnationals to
run subsidiaries, but if the rotation is understood as global management training, resentment of the nonnational boss is minimized.
There are other benefits to rotation too. The corporation is able to
utilize managers from all over the world in whatever positions they
best fit. Furthermore, morale in the subsidiaries is sometimes
higher because managers there see opportunities beyond their own
borders. Firms like 3M and Dow Chemical use management
rotation regularly to build up a core of international managers. Not
everyone likes to be moved around the globe, however. Some

managers like the opportunity when they are early in their careers, but not when they have to worry about children's schooling and other family matters. It is also expensive. Expatriate managers usually get paid a premium for living abroad or get their living accommodation paid. Family trips back home are often part of the package too. Building a global management team leads to some expensive traditions in corporate culture.

Change the Performance-Measurement System to Fit the Mandate

Under the traditional multinational structure country managers had broad strategic autonomy over corporate activities in the country and could therefore reasonably be evaluated on the basis of results. Broad measures of growth and return on invested capital were appropriate. However, to hold a manager responsible for results after his autonomy is reduced is more problematic. The company, of course, is more interested in its overall global results than in the results of any one subsidiary, but if results are to be used to measure a manager's performance, they must somehow fit the mandate assigned to the manager. To take an earlier illustration as an example, if a country manager obtains a mandate requiring some products to be made for world markets, some to be made for the domestic market only, and some to be imported, how is the manager's performance to be evaluated? There is no simple answer, but in general, performance measurement should follow the mandate. In the example cited, three different systems may be required. Normal growth and return-on-investment criteria might apply to products made for the domestic market only. Imported products may be better with a system that measures sales growth by market segment. Products made for world markets may require a system that evaluates quality, cost and delivery only. On the other hand, if the subsidiary has the marketing assignment for its global products, the measurement system might include growth of export sales.

Clearly, globalization leads to more complex measurement systems. That is because responsibility is divided in different ways.

Being responsible to sell a product designed for the global market at a price set by the head office is quite different from selling a domestically designed product at a price set at home. Measurement systems have to reflect these changes in responsibility. They are complicated further by transfer prices on intercorporate trade, and intercorporate trade increases significantly under globalization. Transfer prices are influenced to a limited degree by tax and currency considerations, and some companies eliminate them from the performance-measurement system. Other companies set them on a formula basis to share the profit between production and marketing regardless of which country is shipping to which. Less arbitrary transfer prices of this kind often do not need to be eliminated for performance-measurement purposes.

IS STRUCTURAL CHANGE ENOUGH?

The idea that the best way for American firms to compete against the Japanese is to circulate a new organizational chart would provoke guffaws of derision in American corporate boardrooms. Nevertheless, many American firms are taking a closer look at their organizations because they are anxious to change their approach to competition. At stake are improvements in product cost and quality, customer service and corporate learning. These are areas that do matter, and organizational change can affect them.

Improvements in product cost and quality increasingly require improved product design, specialized production facilities and automated production processes all geared to world markets. It is difficult to get consistent quality in all major markets when autonomous subsidiary executives insist on local adaptation and local production. Cutting back on their autonomy is critical to improving product cost and quality worldwide, and changing the organization's structure is the best way to rein in their autonomy.

Cultivating an attitude of customer service in an organization is no easy task. Organizations that have such an attitude ingrained in their culture always make tough competitors. Getting it ingrained takes consistent effort over time. A shared sense of corporate mission is a useful starting point, but it is not so much the document alone that helps but the level of real commitment to it on the part of top executives. Getting managers to buy into it in various parts of the world is also necessary, and it is easier to do that the more those managers are moved around in the organization. The longer a manager stays in his own country handling only domestic operations, the harder it is for him to identify with the global aspirations of the parent.

When Xerox was up against a major challenge from Japan in photocopiers, Xerox executives found answers in their Japanese joint venture to help them fight back. Westinghouse found that its Canadian affiliate had taken the technological lead in selected gas turbines and was ready to supply and market them worldwide. For many large corporations, their international affiliates are not really subsidiaries at all. They are partners in an international challenge. They participate in the formulation of global strategies as well as in their execution. Information flows two ways, not just from parent to subsidiary. Unfortunately, it has taken many corporations a long time to realize that they can indeed learn from their subsidiaries. Information gathering in these firms has taken second place to information dissemination. However, as Europe and Japan emerge as powerful economic rivals to North America, many observers are suggesting that the successful international firms of the future will have to have a presence in all three markets. Behind this suggestion is the view that it is dangerous for American firms not to know what is going on in Europe and Japan, either in terms of technology or market demand. The same is true for European or Japanese firms in their nondomestic markets.

To what extent can a firm stay in touch with critical competitive information by having subsidiaries or affiliates in key markets? Better than not having affiliates there is the quick answer. But the problem runs deeper than that. Two other things are necessary before a corporation is likely to learn from its affiliates. The first is an open communication channel and an insistence on knowing on the part of senior head-office executives. There has to be a thirst for knowledge at the top, a magnet that pulls in information from all important areas of the world. On the evidence, the Japanese are better at learning than American and European firms. All those groups of Japanese that used to visit American and European factories so deferentially knew what they were looking for. Their bosses back home were clearly interested in the information. The evidence is that so much of it showed up in the kinds of products and processes subsequently developed in Japan. For the most part, there has not been the same commitment to learning on the part of European and American firms, only on the part of individuals. Not many American teams have gone to visit Japanese organizations. Many individuals have, but too often what they have learned has never been internalized by the firm.

The second requirement for effective learning from international affiliates is executives of stature in those affiliates. Firms must have good people abroad and enough people at home who have been abroad before a meaningful dialogue can take place. It is much easier to accomplish this if people are moved around between affiliates and between the head office and the affiliates. A shared sense of corporate mission and a clearer view of who in the organization needs to know a given piece of information tends to emerge from the periodic moving of key people. The other side of the coin is that good people will not stay long in an affiliate without an interesting mandate. If a firm reins in the autonomy of a subsidiary too severely under the globalization imperative, that subsidiary will not be able to keep good people. It will soon dry up as a source of competitive information and as a source of executive talent. This is an important issue. Globalization may well turn out to be a short-sighted policy for those firms who use it primarily to cut costs and centralize power in the head office.

The point is that structural change is not in itself going to make a firm internationally competitive. What will make a difference are improvements in product cost and quality, improvements in customer service and improvements in the firm's ability to learn over time. Changes in corporate structure can influence these things. But there is quite clearly a balancing act involved, and the balancing act centers on the level of autonomy in international affiliates and the role and mandate of international affiliates in the overall corporation. If it were simpler, businesses could be successfully run from a golf-cart computer on the eighteenth hole.

HOW MUCH SUBSIDIARY AUTONOMY CAN BE TOLERATED?

Throughout this chapter the point has been made that globalization, from a parent perspective, means reining in the power of subsidiaries abroad. In industries where scale efficiencies are more significant than the need for local responsiveness, subsidiary power can be reined in more severely. Improvements in product cost and quality are easier to achieve with strong central control. The cost of excessive central control, however, is potentially serious. Overseas affiliates cease to provide a flow of executive talent and useful information to the head office. Because of these difficulties, a number of larger firms have tried to find ways to achieve the efficiency benefits of globalization without emasculating their subsidiaries abroad. Their search has led them to examine the transnational rather than the global approach. As discussed earlier in this chapter, the distinguishing features of the transnational approach are subtle and elusive but potentially very important. The

Table 4.2
Contrasting International Structures

	GLOBAL STRUCTURE	TRANSNATIONAL STRUCTURE	MULTINATIONAL STRUCTURE
PRODUCT LINE	specialized	specialized	duplicated
MARKET EMPHASIS	international	both	national
TRANSFERS	product	product and knowledge	technology and skills
EVALUATION MODE	cost center	varied	profit center
SUBSIDIARY ROLE	implement strategy	participate in formulation of strategy	develop and implement strategy
SUBSIDIARY AUTONOMY	low	medium	high
SUBSIDIARY MANAGEMENT	foreign, short-term	foreign, medium-term	local, long-term

transnational approach can tolerate more subsidiary autonomy than the global approach, and sometimes, though not always, the increased tolerance is vital. It is useful, therefore, to conclude this chapter by contrasting the transnational approach with the global and multinational approaches discussed earlier (table 4.2).

The transnational structure is clearly an in-between approach. If it actually results in an optimal blend of efficiency and local responsiveness, it is clearly better than either the global or the multinational approach. But to define it in terms of the desired result is to make the other two seem like straw men. Rather than argue the theoretical merits of the transnational approach, however, let us at this juncture simply concede that it makes us think more about the role of overseas subsidiaries and how they can contribute usefully to overall corporate objectives. The next chapter looks at globalization from a subsidiary point of view.

NOTE

1. Christopher A. Bartlett and Sumantra Ghoshal, *Managing across Borders: The Transnational Solution* (Boston: Harvard Business School Press, 1989).

5

THE IMPACT OF GLOBALIZATION ON SUBSIDIARIES AND LOCAL FIRMS

Before declining tariffs made globalization possible, subsidiaries used to compete in host countries against local firms. It was common then to attribute the success of subsidiaries to their ability to import technology and other skills efficiently from their parents. Local firms had either to develop their own competing technology in-house, or license it across the market. And because local firms often limited themselves to local markets, they seldom had the sales base to develop their own technology. Licensing was common in Canada. In general, subsidiaries were winning the competitive battle for market share against local firms.

The pressures emanating from the globalization of competition will hit both subsidiaries and local firms, but in different ways. Both will have to adjust. They will no longer be competing so much against one another as against their parents and other global players. The challenges facing both of them are sobering indeed. For subsidiaries the challenges are essentially organizational, whereas for local firms they are essentially strategic and market-based. This chapter will discuss the challenges separately, but this does not mean that the strategic suggestions given to one are altogether irrelevant to the other. The challenge after all has the same origin and, while the responses have to be different, there is certainly some opportunity for common learning.

THE CHALLENGE TO SUBSIDIARIES

Far-reaching changes in product strategy and organizational structure are unavoidable for most international subsidiaries, and particularly for Canadian subsidiaries. The twin pressures of globalization and free trade are forcing the pace of change. Many American parents, however, are leaving it up to their Canadian subsidiaries to take the initiative. The reason for this is that most parents see globalization in terms of Japan and Europe 1992 rather than Canada; the reality of the Free Trade Agreement is still sinking in. At the same time parent-company reluctance provides an opportunity to subsidiary executives to influence the outcome. This chapter therefore focusses on the subsidiary's perspective on globalization. It looks first at the need for change in the status quo, the options available to subsidiaries and their impact on subsidiary culture. Then some suggestions are made to subsidiary executives about managing the transitional period and dealing with minority local shareholders.

Before we proceed, however, it is worth pointing out that foreign direct investment and acquisitions in the United States rose sharply during the 1980s. In fact, the 1990s began with the startling news that the stock of foreign investment in the United States exceeded the stock of American investment abroad. Of course, the investment coming into the United States is more recent than the investment going out. The value of U.S. assets held abroad is still likely to be much higher than the value of foreign assets held in the United States. The trend, however, is important. The number of foreign subsidiaries in the United States is growing. Looking at life through the eyes of subsidiaries is not an exclusively Canadian preoccupation. It is something Americans may have to learn more about. Nevertheless, this chapter has been written from the conventional perspective of American parents with Canadian subsidiaries. After all, for Canada, subsidiaries account for about half of all business activity. Subsidiaries in the United States may be growing, but they have a long way to go before they reach Canadian levels. Indeed, it is entirely possible that Americans will never allow them to reach Canadian levels. Tolerance for foreign investors may not be the same in the two countries. Either way, it is likely over the next decade that the perspective of the subsidiary will get a more understanding hearing in the United States.

SUBSIDIARY CONCERNS ABOUT GLOBALIZATION

Globalization is intimidating from a subsidiary's perspective. It brings with it shades of the past: a danger that insensitive parent companies will impose ill-fitting products and strategies on increasingly dependent subsidiaries. Subsidiary autonomy is something that has been fought for both by subsidiaries and by host governments. Many host governments in Africa, South America, Eastern Europe and the Far East still insist that foreign investors accept joint-venture partners. Part of their purpose is to learn technology and management skills through joint ventures, but the other part is to ensure locally responsive subsidiaries. Many countries that have not insisted on joint ventures have required or encouraged foreign subsidiaries to sell some shares to the public. Their purpose has been to increase the reporting requirements of the subsidiary, to make the subsidiary legally accountable to host-country shareholders and to place local nationals on boards of directors to represent the local shareholders and influence subsidiary policies. These ownership devices have made it easier for host governments to accept and live with the enormous amounts of foreign investment flowing into their countries. They provide an important element of political control over a significant portion of the economy that might otherwise escape that control.

Globalization, however, is challenging this entire approach. Local ownership is an impediment to an integrated global strategy, and many global corporations have been quietly buying back their local shares. Nations that have insisted on joint ventures have been losing their share of foreign investment, and many—Mexico being the most recent example—are relaxing their insistence. Increasingly, international cooperation and interdependence under globalization are seen by many as a safer, more rational approach than excessive nation-state autonomy. The globalization phenomenon, from this perspective, reflects a more mature political accommodation to the shrinking global village.

THE NEED FOR CHANGE

In spite of their concerns about globalization, most subsidiary executives know that change is necessary. Traditionally, subsidiaries have produced multiple products in small-scale facilities for their own domestic market. This strategy was profitable because the subsidiaries were insulated from global competition by tariffs and were supported by their parent companies with a continuous flow of proven, inexpensive product know-how. As tariff barriers come down under free trade, these subsidiaries will lose their special protection and become vulnerable to offshore competition. They will be forced to become competitive by global standards. Achieving global competitiveness will mean withdrawing from their small-scale, generalist approach and specializing in those aspects of the business in which they can maintain a genuine competitive edge.

Westinghouse's recent experiences in Canada illustrate the kind of transformation that subsidiaries must undertake. The firm attempted in 1976 to sell its Canadian major-appliance operations to WCI following the parent company's decision to do the same, but Canada's Foreign Investment Review Agency refused to approve the sale. Without parent-company support the Canadian appliance division would have dwindled, so Westinghouse Canada sold it at a lower price to a Canadian firm. The experience caused the subsidiary to take a closer look at its dependence on its parent. At that time Westinghouse Canada was a large net importer dependent on the parent company for operating technology; costs were high because it produced many of the parent company's products, but in smaller-scale facilities. In many ways Westinghouse Canada was typical of U.S.-owned subsidiaries in tariff-protected environments. It was a miniature replica of its parent.

By the mid-1980s Westinghouse Canada had become an innovative, outward-looking net exporter with internationally competitive costs. It made this transition by specializing in a particular product—a gas turbine—that was based on Canadian R & D and appealed to a worldwide market. Accomplishing this was the result of a very deliberate decision. Westinghouse had a long-standing interest in gas turbines. The Canadian subsidiary selected a particular size of turbine and improved its design through R & D activity within Canada. Having done so, it earned the right to sell its product worldwide either directly or through the Westinghouse sales force.

Managing the transition turned out to be tougher than expected, however. The task was to make the Canadian subsidiary more like a U.S. division, and doing so required some important changes in corporate culture. A subsidiary that has long been dependent on home-office technological expertise and a captive local market does not become innovative and international overnight. Because the Canadian product was important to other divisions in Westinghouse, the Canadian CEO had to take his place in the central strategic committees of the parent alongside U.S. division managers. Initially this was achieved by sending a strong U.S. executive to run the Canadian operation. The plan was to groom a Canadian for the role, but it took several years to do this.

TWO FORMS OF SPECIALIZATION

Westinghouse Canada specialized by developing and marketing a product with worldwide appeal, one that did not replicate its parent company's products. This is the world-product-mandate approach. Rationalization, by contrast, usually takes the form of a negotiated agreement between parent and subsidiary to let the subsidiary produce a selected product or component for world markets in return for its importing other products from the parent or from other subsidiaries. Both approaches produce the manufacturing efficiencies associated with specialization, and both result in a product line produced on a world-scale basis. Despite these similarities, they add value in very different ways.

Using a rationalization strategy, the subsidiary becomes a factor rather than a division, a cost center rather than a profit center and integrated rather than autonomous. The U.S. automobile industry in Canada is a straightforward example. The subsidiaries produce largely for U.S. demand and take their instructions down to model product design, colors and output volumes from U.S. executives. The parent manufacturing facilities also produce largely for the U.S. market, so Canadian marketing executives exert little influence. This situation is not so much a power grab by U.S. executives as it is a natural consequence of a rationalization strategy: the country with the large market dominates the strategy. Both parent and subsidiary are managed with the demands of the parent market in mind.

A subsidiary operating under a world-product-mandate strategy becomes more like a division of the parent. Like any vibrant division, it plays a role in the strategic decision making of the enterprise. The subsidiary still specializes and gains the efficiencies of world-scale production, but it does not trade its soul to get them. At the heart of the concept is subsidiary responsibility for international marketing and product renewal (product design and improvements as well as process technology). The two cannot be separated. Product renewal is unmanageable if the subsidiary is not also responsible for international marketing; successful R & D must be shaped by a thorough knowledge of consumer needs. The fact that subsidiaries must be responsible for international marketing does not imply that they are independent of the corporation's international sales force, however. On the contrary, there must be an ongoing, dynamic interchange between the two. Strong product divisions have long been accustomed to this interdependence, but most subsidiaries have not.

How should a firm choose between rationalization and a world-product-mandate approach? How should specific products be selected for specialized production? As a general rule, rationalization agreements are negotiated, while world product mandates are earned.

Rationalization

Parent-company production facilities are generally more affected by this strategy, because rationalization means adjustment to parent output to compensate for subsidiary specialization: slight increases in parent output for products dropped by the subsidiary and a sharp drop in parent output of the product chosen for subsidiary specialization. There is a real aversion to shutting down U.S. factories to accommodate specialization in Canada or overseas; as a result, many agreements involve the production either of component parts or of products in the late life-cycle stages. Producing component parts has the virtue of insulating the subsidiary from fluctuations of customer demand for particular models. Hence it may create more stable employment arrangements for both sides. GE Canada's blade and vane plant in Bromont, Quebec, for example, was built to supply parts for aero engines made in the United States for GE. The agreement gave the parent company certain defense offset benefits as well. From Canada's perspective, the arrangement provided steady employment in a "super high-tech" environment.

U.S.-Canadian rationalization agreements frequently involve mature products because Canadian subsidiaries can manage small-volume production more efficiently, so a product line can run out its useful life more profitably in Canada. The reason is that Canada, like other small-market economies, is more experienced than the United States in small-volume production. Mature products are also assigned to Canada because U.S. divisions are reluctant to cede control of growth products that they have nursed through the demanding innovative years. When rationalization takes the form of assigning mature products, the arrangement must be reviewed frequently. The subsidiary operation grows increasingly dependent over time, but fundamental cost comparisons will drive the process as long as actual plant shutdowns are unnecessary.

World Product Mandate

Whether a particular subsidiary should hold a world product mandate depends on the initiative and managerial depth of the subsidiary and on the style and culture of its parent. These mandates are usually "earned" in the sense that the parent company must have confidence in the subsidiary's ability to manage the growth of the product in question. That confidence is earned most readily when the original product innovation is developed in the subsidiary—as in the case of Westinghouse Canada's gas turbine—or when the subsidiary becomes by its own efforts, or by acquisition, the best source of that technology within the enterprise. Quite often when a subsidiary has a world product mandate, the product is simply not made anywhere else in the enterprise and never has been. Mandates often involve newer products. When this is the case, the future of the subsidiary rests in its own hands, which may or may not suit the style and culture of the parent corporation.

THE IMPACT OF SPECIALIZATION ON SUBSIDIARY CULTURE

The challenge to subsidiary managers facing globalization pressures is to avoid, if possible, the rationalization of the whole subsidiary. The rationalized subsidiary is the counterpart of the global structure with its accent on efficiency ahead of local adaptiveness. The miniature replica subsidiary, of course, is the counterpart of the multinational structure and is hence the form most under threat from globalization. The world-product-mandate subsidiary is, more or less, the counterpart of the transnational structure, which attempts both efficiency gains and local adaptiveness through strong subsidiaries with life-giving mandates. Parent companies will make their choice of strategy and structure, as discussed in chapter 4, on the basis of globalization pressures division by division. It is the subsidiary manager's challenge to influence these choices one by one by emphasizing the capacity and depth of the subsidiary relative to the roles it might play. If a division-by-division, product-by-product analysis results in a mixed bag —that is, between product mandate, rationalization and miniature replica—then the subsidiary manager has to learn how to manage a "mixed-bag" subsidiary.

In firms like GE, Honeywell and 3M the relationship between parent and subsidiary depends on the division in question. Take, for example, GE Canada's blade and vane plant in Quebec. There is no possibility of GE Canada getting into the aero-engine business, so that facility is rationalized. The product specifications and design engineering are done of necessity in the United States. The minimization of costs within quality constraints is the critical task for the Quebec plant. This does not, however, mean that GE Canada as a whole is rationalized. Its appliance division, Camco, with minority Canadian shareholders of its own, is still in the process of working out its preferred strategy, but it is doing it product by product. It is also taking the initiative to position itself to be a lead corporate supplier in selected products where the parent company has not invested heavily. Honeywell's Canadian operation earned a mandate some years ago by redesigning one of the parent company's products to reduce its cost and widen its application. However, until a marketing strategy was developed to guide the international sales force, market share outside Canada did not grow very quickly. The Canadian subsidiary had to develop that marketing strategy and motivate the sales force before the "new" product began to reach its international potential. It was an unexpected and unfamiliar challenge to which the subsidiary took some time to respond. On the other hand, when 3M built a new tape factory in Canada to serve the North American market as a whole, the Canadian managers were anxious to start marketing in the United States but were told that their efforts were unnecessary. The U.S. sales force at 3M knew exactly how to market the tape because it was a product they were familiar with. They did not need marketing help.

It does not take much imagination to recognize how damaging rationalization could be to subsidiary culture. If an entire subsidiary were converted to the role of specialized supplier to the parent, the range of skills needed in the subsidiary would diminish accordingly. Many good people would leave. If a subsidiary has little managerial and technological depth to start with, turning it into a rationalized supplier may not constitute much of a loss. But if it does have managerial and technological depth, it will soon lose this depth if it is rationalized. Furthermore, it would not be easy to get it back. Rationalization is a one-way ticket to decline for subsidiaries because it leaves them with insufficient creative scope to hold on to good people. Subsidiary CEOs will therefore resist it whenever they sensibly can. In some divisions there is no reasonable alternative. In divisions where there is a reasonable alternative, subsidiary managers simply have to learn to position themselves to take advantage of it. The idea that subsidiary managers can in fact influence the outcome by positioning themselves intelligently within the firm as a whole is not exactly revolutionary, but it is probably better understood in the field than in the head office. What kinds of initiatives can subsidiary managers reasonably take? What can they do to manage the transition to globalization effectively from a subsidiary perspective? It is to these issues that we now turn.

MANAGING THE TRANSITION

It is essential that subsidiary managers set their strategies to contribute to the welfare of the company as a whole. There is no point in trying to insist on subsidiary autonomy for no good reason, and no point in setting a strategic course at variance with that of the parent organization. The challenge is to carve a useful role consistent with the parent's strategy by which the subsidiary can make a genuine and perhaps unique contribution to the overall global thrust of the firm. Subsidiary managers who try jealously to preserve their independence for nationalistic reasons are not likely to survive long. Subsidiaries simply have to understand the strategic thrust of their parents, product by product, division by division, and then carve out a sensible strategic role that does not duplicate parent activity. By sensible we mean a role for which the subsidiary is equipped in terms of managerial and technological depth and a role in which the subsidiary is competitive within the enterprise. A first step, therefore, in managing the transition to globalization from a subsidiary standpoint is to examine parent-company strategy. Only then is it possible to work out what role the subsidiary might play.

Examine the Parent's Strategy

At one level the subsidiary should examine the company's product line to determine whether the nature of demand differs between the Canadian and American markets. If it does, it is not hard to make the case that shifting operations to the United States will damage market share in Canada over time. Take major appliances as an illustration. Because of sizeable scale economies in production, major appliances would appear to be a prime candidate for rationalization. However, there are several differences between the Canadian and U.S. markets. Canadians are more fashion-conscious about kitchen appliances, and standard U.S. range designs would not capture Canadian consumers. Portable dishwashers are a bigger seller in Canada than in the United States, as are chest-type freezers. Washing machines may be about to go electronic, in which case the market on both sides of the border may be turbulent. The more different the markets, the stronger the case for retaining some production in Canada and some autonomy in Canadian operations.

At another level subsidiary managers should examine parent-company strengths and weaknesses in order to work out an appropriate subsidiary role. It makes little sense for the subsidiary manager to duplicate its parent's R & D effort. The trick is for the subsidiary to concentrate on a unique or overlooked product area. Sometimes the Canadian operation can take on part of an integrated research task by agreement with the parent. A case in point is Xerox Canada. The parent has established three principal R & D facilities in the world; one is located in Canada. This facility has a mandate to carry out basic and applied research involving imaging processing. This includes work in paper, toner and photoreceptor technology. Much of this work is initiated by Xerox facilities outside Canada. The Canadian R & D facility is fully integrated within the entire corporation and is somewhat independent of the strategic interests of Xerox Canada.

More interestingly, subsidiaries can also initiate work on products in which the parent has not yet invested and develop a special expertise in those products. An example of this is Motorola Canada. The research and development group of Motorola Canada employs about 100 persons in two Toronto-area locations. This group assists the subsidiary's Communications Group, which has established a world product mandate for the design, manufacture and sale of a series of land mobile radio products and systems. The mandate for two-way radios lends itself to a specialty niche in the twenty-five–to thirty-five–watt segment of the industry. Motorola Canada's Product Operations group also controls the mandate for the design, manufacture and world marketing of computer communications equipment, including modems and data multiplexers. Much of this mandate was assumed by Motorola Canada after it proved to the parent that it was able to assert control over product development as well as manufacturing and international sales.

Naturally, such initiatives should be openly discussed with the parent, because if they are successful, they serve as reinforcement to the parent of the subsidiary's competence. If the subsidiary wants to attract and hold good people, project initiatives are important. Without them the technical capacity of the subsidiary soon diminishes.

Examine the Subsidiary's Strengths and Weaknesses

Subsidiary managers should examine their own strengths and weaknesses product by product and compare them to those of their parent and to other subsidiaries around the world. It is also important for subsidiaries to communicate their strengths clearly to their parent. What the parent thinks of the subsidiary is in some ways more important than what the subsidiary thinks of itself. Major projects are subject to competition within international firms. Canadian subsidiaries find themselves competing with other subsidiaries and sometimes with parent divisions for projects. Relative production costs play an important role in the competition, but often the quality reputation and technological depth of the subsidiary are more important. A good example of this is Ingersoll-Rand Canada, which was involved in bidding for a dramatic expansion of its role in the company's global pump operations. However, the subsidiary first had to convince its parent of its superior cost and quality reputation vis-à-vis other affiliates.

Subsidiary managers need to think in terms of positioning their subsidiary to become the "natural leader" in selected products within the corporation. Positioning implies extensive knowledge about what the subsidiary is good at and what the parent is not. It implies a gradual buildup of expertise through small studies, miniature research projects, pilot production in existing facilities, and testing market acceptance domestically. The accumulation of expertise and the seizing of well-thought-out initiatives are at the heart of positioning the subsidiary within the corporation. The process is ongoing. Repositioning in the light of changing patterns of demand and technology is important too. When the process stops, the subsidiary starts to die. The challenge is to stay one step ahead of a moving target.

The case of Cyanamid Canada is illustrative in this regard. In the early 1980's its parent undertook a dramatic shift in corporate strategy to reposition itself as a "research oriented biotechnology and specialty chemical company." What followed was a series of divestitures that led to the downsizing of much of Cyanamid Canada's operations from a peak of 3,000 employees to 1,400 by 1989. Canadian executives, anxious to reestablish a growth pattern for their operations, felt that the subsidiary's competitive advantage lay in producing smaller-run products that required high levels of technological input. Consequently, in 1988 Cyanamid Canada began focussing efforts on reaching out to new technologies in highly specialized fields where it could best apply its unique strengths, resulting in two acquisitions of Canadian biotechnology companies. Both acquisitions provided the subsidiary with considerable control over operations and an opportunity to learn skills that will enable it to pursue world product mandates in the future consistent with the parent's overall strategy.

Determine Canada's Strengths

When the battle for projects or product mandates is on, what unique appeals do subsidiary managers in Canada make to support their bids? Is there anything Canadian subsidiaries tend to do cheaper or better than their parents? While generalizations are always dangerous, there are some areas of expertise that are frequently mentioned by Canadian subsidiary managers.

- Product design and development costs are often lower in Canada, and many Canadian subsidiaries have significant technological depths in-house to undertake design projects.

- Canadians are more accustomed to low-volume production and can handle it at better cost levels than their parents.

- Canadian subsidiaries can handle small export orders more efficiently, especially when product modifications are required. One reason, of course, is that Canadians are more accustomed to low-volume production, but another is that Canadians are more willing to pursue small foreign orders if their parents will let them.

- Canadian subsidiaries can often handle international operations outside of the mainstream developed nations better than their parents because of familiarity with small-volume production and the subsidiary role. Some, as a result, handle Latin America and some Eastern Europe, and so on. Du Pont Canada's CEO has extensive international responsibility for the Du Pont organization as a whole.

Get Closer to the Parent

If globalization requires increased integration between parents and subsidiaries, then subsidiary executives must find ways of learning more about the parent organization. Subsidiaries have to get plugged in on an ongoing basis. This means that subsidiary CEOs have to find their way onto key strategic committees of the parent company. It means that parent appointees on subsidiary boards of directors need to be people of stature from whom subsidiaries can learn. But for the subsidiaries that take integration seriously, it means much more. Du Pont Canada, for example, bought a second airplane to handle the increased traffic back and forth to U.S. operations, not just of the CEO and other top executives but of product managers, R & D staff, design people, plant managers and so on. Du Pont's Canadian executives encouraged a broad flow of people because they wanted the organization to understand what it meant to be competitive within the Du Pont empire. The culture of Du Pont made it possible to have extensive interchange of ideas with no direct threat to the operating authority of the subsidiary. As a result, the subsidiary took the initiative in integration rather than waiting for the parent to impose it.

Develop Unique Products in Subsidiaries

A number of subsidiaries have used their accumulated R & D capacity to develop adaptations of parent products or new related products that have become areas of distinctive competence. It is not unusual for a large subsidiary to have 20 percent of its sales in products its parent does not make. These areas of distinctive competence have sometimes been the basis for world-product-mandate arrangements. It takes, of course, a good deal of subsidiary initiative to build expertise independent of one's parent, but it is precisely this kind of initiative that pays off in terms of autonomy down the road.

Sometimes the subsidiary's expertise is simply the development of a unique model of a product in the parent's line. It may be a top-of-the-line model. In other cases the subsidiary obtains its distinctive competence by licensing-in technology or by acquiring other firms. Subsidiaries with a strong tradition of autonomy may wish to look much more carefully at positioning themselves through acquisition or licensing as globalization and the Free Trade Agreement work their way through the economy. In the past, Canada's Foreign Investment Review Agency was an impediment to subsidiary acquisitions, but under its new name, Investment Canada, it no longer is. Subsidiary managers that have forgotten what it is like to hit the acquisition trail may have to rebuild their skills.

Remember That You Are the Subsidiary

There is always a danger when recommending strategic initiatives to subsidiaries. Handled badly, they can easily cause a quick exit from the company. No subsidiary is going to make an acquisition without its parent's approval. The reality is that subsidiary initiative is more acceptable in some areas of activity than in others. Every firm is different, of course, but if a subsidiary wants to understand when to take strategic initiatives and when to take orders, figure 5.1 might help.

Figure 5.1 suggests that subsidiaries should be careful about taking initiatives. First they should assess their own capability in the area in question; then they should assess the parent's capability. As a rule, the parent's competence to act in the subsidiary's market will depend on whether the subsidiary's market is significantly different from what the parent is used to (that is, high localization

Figure 5.1
Subsidiary Competence and Subsidiary Initiative

	Low subsidiary capability	High subsidiary capability
High localization pressures	form alliances or make acquisitions	take strategic initiative
High globalization pressures	follow parent instructions	influence parent strategies

Source: Adapted in part from figure 4.3 and in part from a diagram in Bartlett and Ghoshal, "Tap Your Subsidiaries for Global Reach," *Harvard Business Review*, November–December 1986, 90.

pressures). If it is, and if the subsidiary has a good depth of knowledge in the area, it should provide strategic leadership. If neither the parent nor the subsidiary has the necessary competence, the company should either get out of the segment or the subsidiary should try to build capability, perhaps by alliance or acquisition. In product areas where globalization potential prevails, parent-company expertise will be relevant in the subsidiary's market. When the subsidiary's technological and market knowledge is low relative to the parent's—that is, in conditions of rationalization—the subsidiary should simply follow parent-company direction. However, when the subsidiary's competence is also high—that is, in conditions of product mandate—the subsidiary should try to influence parent strategy.

The subsidiary management, whether taking strategic initiative or following parent instructions, absolutely has to be well plugged in at headquarters. It is not a good idea to presume the competence level of the parent in a given product area. One has to know. At the same time it is not a good idea to make an acquisition or take a strategic initiative without prior parent approval. Taking initiative is not the same as declaring independence. It is interdependence that is needed, and interdependence requires a measure of integration and working together. Taking the initiative in an interdependent relationship means bringing ideas and plans to the key management committees and championing them. Success is achieved through the quality of the ideas and through the competence with which they are expressed, but also through the preconditioning of other executives present. That is why it is so important for subsidiary managers to be well plugged in at headquarters. They need to understand the mind-set of the other executives, and they need opportunities to influence it.

MINORITY SHAREHOLDERS IN CANADIAN SUBSIDIARIES

Quite a number of Canadian subsidiaries have a degree of local ownership of their shares. A brief review of the 1988 *Financial*

Post top 500 Canadian businesses disclosed that 203 of them were subsidiaries. Of the 203 subsidiaries, 136 were wholly owned, and 67 had minority shareholders. Recently there have been several buyouts by parents of the minority shareholders in their Canadian subsidiaries. Nabisco bought out its minority shareholders. Imperial Chemical Industries (ICI) bought out the minority shareholders in Canadian Industries Limited (CIL), as did Tate and Lyle in Redpath. In 1989 GE announced that it was taking GE Canada private with the purchase of its 8 percent public shareholdings. Stockbrokers in Canada publish lists of subsidiaries with traded shares suggesting that impending parent buyouts make them a good buy. Minority ownership seems threatened by globalization. It is not difficult to see the nature of the threat.

The purpose of minority public shareholders from a host-country perspective was to increase the accountability of subsidiaries. This was to be achieved through the legal accountability firms have to their shareholders, through the increased reporting requirements associated with going public and through outsider representation on the subsidiary's board of directors. Underlying these requirements was the view that subsidiaries should be "Canadianized" a bit and made more responsive to local concerns and opportunities. Globalization in its pure form would challenge the need for these extraneous localization pressures. With tariffs gone, the need for localization of subsidiaries is reduced. Furthermore, globalization leads to greater intercorporate trade, and transfer prices between units with unequal ownership can be troublesome. GE's recent purchase of its minority shareholdings is a case in point. With the increase in globalization, GE received more than 35 percent of its profits from international sales in 1989. Furthermore, the company vowed that it would be either number one or number two in each of the businesses in which it competed, or it would get out. This placed considerable pressure on GE Canada, which had been the only subsidiary in the corporation with minority shareholdings. The problem was that Canadian-responsiveness was not always compatible with corporate objectives. In commenting on the challenges facing the subsidiary, William Blundell, chairman of GE

Canada, was quoted in the June 19, 1989, edition of the *Globe and Mail* as saying: "Our strategy over the last five years has been to move away from a miniature GE, which is a polite name for a branch plant operation, to being a player in the global GE team. . . . [This can be best achieved where we can] add value from a Canadian base." Spending $118 million to buy out the remaining publicly held equity was viewed as an attempt to centralize control of the subsidiary and thereby facilitate specialization efforts.

The flip side of globalization is loss of local autonomy—a move away from subsidiary independence—and strong local boards can be an impediment in this process. Some subsidiary managers use the argument of local shareholder rights to resist parent-company strategic moves they do not like. What is troubling some businesses even more is that globalization has led to many foreign acquisitions and alliances. Parents frequently end up with the Canadian subsidiaries of recently acquired firms that were wholly owned at the time of acquisition, and they are reluctant to turn them over to their own Canadian subsidiaries where their ownership is reduced by minority shareholders. What is more, when a parent company gets into certain kinds of international alliances, the rights of its subsidiaries to share in the benefits often require separate agreements.

On a number of dimensions it is clear that minority public shareholdings in subsidiaries constitute an impediment to the globalization process. On the other hand, the need for subsidiaries to be open and responsive with host governments is not entirely a thing of the past. One subsidiary executive put it this way: "I think all subsidiaries should have local ownership. It makes the company more transparent and keeps it out of trouble in the long run. Canada should have economic incentives in place to encourage more local ownership in subsidiaries."

The arguments in favor of local ownership are the same as the arguments favoring local autonomy in subsidiaries, and local autonomy is clearly one of the casualties of globalization. However, the transnational approach, with its accent on maintaining strong subsidiaries with significant mandates, may not be entirely at odds with maintaining local shareholders. Subsidiaries with strong local boards have an easier time attracting and holding good people and an easier time taking initiatives and developing distinctive competences. Without local ownership it is too easy to clone obedient subsidiaries. In life, parents let go of their children as they mature; otherwise the relationship between them becomes strained. In business, parents run a similar risk with excessively dependent subsidiaries.

The real question is whether subsidiaries with minority share-holders can make the journey from independence to interdependence. Even transnational subsidiaries are more integrated than multinational subsidiaries. How might the integration process be managed? Certainly some subsidiaries with minority-interest share-holders have managed to become well plugged in and thoroughly aligned with parent-company strategies. Will minority share-holders be a benefit in the long run? It is hard to say, but globalization is certainly challenging the need for them, and the battle for their future is on.

THE OVERALL IMPACT OF GLOBALIZATION ON SUBSIDIARIES

Clearly, subsidiary managers stand to lose a lot under globalization. However, they may also gain a lot in unexpected ways. The chief losses and gains are likely to be as follows:

Losses	Gains
Strategic independence	Influence on parent strategies
Local autonomy	Global vision
Generalist scope	Specialist depth
Imported technology	In-house R & D

Effective managers will find ways to minimize the losses and optimize the gains. The best approach to achieve this, simply put, is to run a competitive operation in harmony with overall corporate strategy. Large subsidiaries may end up operating several divisions, each with different linkages to the parent, but no division will survive long if it is not competitive and consistent with corporate needs. Subsidiaries in the future will not be protected havens. The pressure to compete is likely to grow, but if it is met creatively, the result for subsidiary managers could be dramatic indeed. The loss of strategic independence could well turn into a crack at the top job. At least the opportunity is there. It starts with exposure to the top management committees of the parent. For effective managers, exposure turns into influence. Perhaps not many will turn influence into direction, but those who do will blaze a trail for many ambitious subsidiary managers to follow. Globalization is likely to transform the role of subsidiaries. If good people are to be attracted to subsidiaries, the new role must include the possibility of moving to other units in other countries and ultimately the possibility of competing for the top job.

Globalization is leading us toward a less insular, more competitive society. Large international corporations have to find ways to prosper in the midst of greater competitiveness, and one way is to bring a stronger competitiveness ethic into the structure of the corporation itself. In other words, make subsidiaries compete within the overall corporation. Since Canada, under the Free Trade Agreement, has to manage the transition from a protected to a competitive society, it is desirable that subsidiaries should have to do the same thing. But it is also desirable that subsidiaries retain their ability to attract good people, and that means an interdependent relationship with headquarters and a mandate that goes beyond rationalization. It bears repeating that this is a very important issue for Canada because almost half of its economy is accounted for by subsidiaries of foreign—largely American—firms. Unfortunately, rationalization often appears to be the easier route for parents to follow under free trade, but it is a route that limits the future of the subsidiary and seals its dependence on the parent over time. Canada's free trade negotiators saw a different vision. By building the Free Trade Agreement on the national-treatment principle, they sought to maintain two markets with different regulations and procedures and thus lend strength to the role of Canadian subsidiaries. American firms that emasculate their Canadian subsidiaries and try to run their Canadian operations from the United States will probably end up losing market share because of market differences. One of the great challenges facing Canada under free trade is to move from independence to interdependence without slipping into dependence. The same challenge faces Canadian subsidiaries of American firms. To be sure, there are conditions where rationalization is the sensible strategic choice for a particular division, but rationalization of an entire subsidiary may not be good for the future of the parent and certainly will not be good for the future of the subsidiary.

We are on an exciting journey into an ever-smaller world, and international corporations are leading the way. As barriers to trade come down, the discernment and sensitivity of international corporations has to go up. Parent companies need to establish internal conditions keyed to competitiveness that stimulate rather than blunt the creativity of their subsidiaries and affiliates. Subsidiaries need to take imaginative though not necessarily audacious initiative during the transition; for the most part the initiative will be left up to them. They will have an opportunity to play a significant role in the shaping of their own destiny. It will be a difficult role to play. Some corporate cultures do not easily accommodate subsidiary initiative.

THE CHALLENGE TO LOCAL FIRMS

Not all firms are global, though most firms feel the effects of globalization if only in the form of tougher competition at home. What can local firms do in the face of global competition? They can either roll over and die, seek government protection, or develop managerial defense or counterattack strategies. Since protectionism is diminishing, we focus now on the managerial response options facing local firms who are losing market share at home to global competitors. A number of defensive moves can be made to hold on to one's markets. But, there are also counterattack options that can strengthen the firm regionally through alliances. In other words, local firms can do a number of things on their own to make the global competitors' job a lot more difficult.

DEFENDING HOME BASE

The problem for most local firms is that their global competitors have high quality, low cost products as a result of their global specialization. They are hard to underprice, and often hard to outperform in product quality. For many local firms global competition creates a mental block. The challenge is impossible. They approach it totally unprepared by their past experience as local competitors. Those who manage to bring themselves to face the global monster head-on often start to see chinks of strategic daylight filtering through the seemingly impregnable competition. Only then can they start to think about defending their home base.

Strengthen Customer Relations

Why not start out by strengthening relationships with key customers? Building a customer service orientation throughout the firm is an excellent form of defense. It is always more difficult for a foreign competitor to steal a satisfied customer than an alienated one. Of course, it is no easy matter to build a customer service orientation in a firm. It takes commitment from the top and training throughout the ranks. *Forbes* reported in its November 27, 1989 issue that the secret of Huntsman Chemical's early success was that its president and owner, Jon Huntsman, went out to visit customers personally to determine how he could serve them better. He got to know their needs and he got the people in his organization to put customer needs at the top of their priorities. Listening to customers, seeking their feedback and finding out how to help them achieve their objectives are not insurmountable problems. Firms don't need help from governments to do these things.

In Japan, where outsiders face major problems breaking through the distribution channels to reach customers, one of the most intractable difficulties is the closeness and duration of supplier-customer relations. Customers are used to exceptional service from suppliers and long-term relationships with them. In addition, there are rigidities in Japanese distribution systems that make life even more difficult for foreigners. These rigidities are now beginning to loosen, but the close supplier-customer relationships will remain a tough barrier to crack. The suggestion to U.S. and Canadian firms facing global competition is to build similar relationships with their own domestic customers through a total commitment to customer service. Make it more difficult for global competitors to steal customers.

Stay Competitive in Price and Quality

The other challenge to local firms is not to let global competitors get too far ahead in price and quality. Good relations with customers can only do so much. If the price-quality gap between local and global production gets too wide, even well-serviced customers will switch. However, the challenge is not as hopeless as many suppose. What it requires varies by industry, but one essential ingredient is focus on the part of the local firm. It is better to do one or two things well than many things poorly. Focus helps a firm with limited resources stay abreast of technology and develop in-house core skills in its area of specialization. This in turn enables it to learn from license agreements with other firms.

However, while focus helps keep costs down and stimulates R & D, it can cause problems in the marketplace. For the sales force it is often more economical to carry a broader line of products. A heavy investment in customer service is easier to sustain with a broader product line. Where this is the case, one solution is to form marketing alliances with other small focussed manufacturers. When Australia and New Zealand got serious about free trade in 1983, some local firms entered into cross-ownership agreements in order to work together more effectively. What they did was to buy into one another's equity, not to get control, but to sit on one another's boards and coordinate strategy. Other firms simply agreed to handle one another's products in the local markets where they were strong.

What these approaches suggest is that smaller firms do not have to become big to compete against big firms. Smaller firms can try to do through cooperative agreements what global firms routinely do through control. Sometimes they can do it better. It is no easy matter, as we have seen, to manage a global organization effectively. As it happens, developments in computerized manufacturing are limiting the advantages of large scale production. Local firms may not be able to underprice global firms all that often, but they can get close enough that their customer relations will win the day.

It was often argued during the seventies and eighties that large international firms were successful because certain things were easier or cheaper to do in-house than across the market. On this logic, the large firm would always have certain advantages over the small firm, because the small firm would have to transact more often across the market. However, globalization and the information age may be blunting some of the advantages of bigness. Information is now more readily accessible to smaller firms. There is no reason why smaller firms in the nineties will be at quite the same disadvantage against larger firms as they have been in the past. If local firms are managed well, and, particularly if they stay up-to-date in technology and cultivate a customer service orientation, they can defend their home markets more successfully against the global onslaught.

COUNTERATTACKING

As the old sports adage goes, attack is often the best means of defense. One way of dealing with global competitors is to attack them in other world markets. Do not let them concentrate on your market, distract them! Give them no place to hide. This kind of advice usually goes over better in a convention speech than it does in the trenches where the competition really takes place. The problem for the local firm is that it is inexperienced in world markets and often cannot provide a big enough distraction there.

Become a Regional Player

What some North American firms are doing is making the most of their opportunities in the North American market. They are becoming strong regional players with operations in Canada, the

United States and Mexico. In the process they are getting their costs down to global levels and moving swiftly to adopt new technologies. Strong regional players are big enough to attack global firms in third markets and keep them off-balance. There may be many industries in which global players have few advantages over regional players. Competition in these industries may well ultimately take the form of regional players in North America taking on regional players in Europe and the Far East, with none of them exporting much more than 10 percent of their output outside their regions.

In some industries, effective regional players do not have to be all that big to be successful. Globalization is leaving some interesting market niches in its wake. Businesses have more success identifying market niches once they adopt a customer service orientation. A careful study of customer needs often triggers an approach to differentiating a firm's product offerings in ways customers are willing to pay for. For example, in the Huntsman case, as *Forbes* reported, small changes in otherwise commodity chemicals helped certain customers to reduce operating costs. Pursuit of a particular market niche enables a firm to develop a distinctive capability: to learn to serve some particular market need very thoroughly. Some market niches are not global. They may be created by local distribution practices, or other factors specific to the culture of the region. Others may be global, but still many firms prefer to become a strong regional player first and then size up their options elsewhere in the world. They may well decide to license their expertise into other less familiar markets, or to form some kind of alliance with a firm in another region. In other words, a firm does not have to become world scale in order to take advantage of global markets. Now that information is more available through new technologies, cooperative agreements with firms in other regions of the world are less impractical. However, a firm does have to be big enough to have developed a distinctive skill and to maintain and advance that skill over time. The trend of the eighties has been away from trying to compete in many technologies and few countries, toward focussing on key technologies and operating in many countries. Firms have begun to concentrate on what they are really good at. In the process, they have become leaner in terms of administrative staff, and more prone to take action than to hold meetings. Nevertheless, not all players have chosen to become global. Some are remaining regional in focus, and yet striving to take advantage of global opportunities through global alliances rather than direct investment.

Form Global Alliances

Global alliances are formed for many different reasons. Some, as just described, may be formed to market a firm's existing products in unfamiliar markets overseas. Others may be formed to obtain product or process technology from a foreign firm. Yet others may be formed for joint research where research costs are high—as in pharmaceuticals—or for joint design and production where scale economies are significant—as with auto engines or transmissions.

Instinctively, alliances would seem to be the smaller firm's way of competing with bigger firms, or the regional firm's way of going global without the resource commitment of direct investment. But even large firms are getting into alliances. The costs and risks of global innovation and global brand name building have become so high that even the resources of large firms are not enough. Alliances are being sought to share risks and costs. Many Japanese investments in North America are joint ventures as are many American investments in Japan. In the latter case, the Japanese all but required it, but in the former case, it was more by choice. The Japanese have always viewed alliances as an important way of learning. Ultimately, the alliance partner that learns the most from the alliance will end up dominating it.

In many alliances with large organizations, there is some kind of equity position taken by each partner in the other. Some firms view alliances as a way of sizing up the quarry before launching a takeover. They are more interested in control than in learning. Smaller firms view global alliances as a necessity for surviving in a shrinking world. They are convinced, or have to be by virtue of their size, that beneficial learning is possible without control; that firms can stay small and still be global through mutually beneficial alliances. The Canadian company ISC that has developed the IMAX large screen movie technology is an interesting illustration. The company is staying small and developing internationally by working almost entirely with alliance partners. Every IMAX movie has a corporate sponsor to defray production costs. Every IMAX theatre has an investor who owns and manages it. ISC focusses on the technology, its basic strength. It has resisted the temptation to grow big by doing things, such as operating theatres, that it is not especially good at.

Alliances, of course, do not always run smoothly. They can be difficult to manage. But managed well they present an opportunity for small niche players to go global profitably without inheriting all the difficulties of running a global organization. Firms like ISC are learning that it is possible by maintaining a sharp focus on one's real competitive advantage, to exploit that advantage successfully in the world through cooperative alliances, while reducing both the risks, and the financial and managerial commitment required to do everything oneself.

The Overall Impact of Globalization on Local Firms

Bigness and economic control across borders are not necessarily corollaries of globalization. Control brings one set of problems and alliances another. In a global information era, learning may well turn out to be more important than control. Smaller firms who become regional players may well be powerful enough to defend their markets from global competitors, as long as they develop a strong customer service orientation and stay reasonably up-to-date in technology, quality and cost. They may also make occasional forays overseas to keep their competitors off-balance, but not with the same intensity that they use to defend their home base.

Smaller firms can also participate in global markets by forming alliances with foreign firms, and by using alliances of different kinds to substitute for having to invest themselves. In this way, they not only stay relatively small, they also stay very focussed on their real strategic strengths. Many large firms during the eighties have been questioning the value of excessive control, except for the leveraged buy out specialists from whom it is the only game that counts. A lot of large firms have been downsizing, cutting out excessive administration, contracting out more tasks and sometimes selling off whole businesses. Behind these moves is the recognition that it is hard to compete in global terms unless you focus enough to do things really well. Size to some large firms has become an impediment. In the interest of control, they have done too many things in-house, not always efficiently. They are starting to weed them out, hoping to increase profits by increasing focus and shrinking size. The global Goliaths of the future may not be as big as people expect. In fact, size and control may not be as important in the knowledge era ahead as cooperation and learning. The smaller more focussed and more nimble firms may well embarrass the global giants in world markets, just as the Lilliputians swarmed all over the impotent Gulliver.

6

THE FUTURE HAS ARRIVED

Canada and the United States are in the early stages of a marriage, and the early stages are when most of the adjustment difficulties usually come to the surface. Difficulties, of course, are only to be expected and certainly can be managed when both parties are paying attention. American attention, however, is being diverted—not surprisingly—by activity in Europe and Japan. Global productivity data show that the United States has been falling behind in productivity growth for over ten years. The success of Japan in world markets is a natural outcome of decades of productivity enhancement. What is really surprising Americans is Japan's capacity to develop new and better products and its dedication to the knowledge-based industries. Anything to do with the development, transmission, storage or display of information attracts Japan's attention. These have been the growth areas of the eighties and, arguably, the precipitators of globalization with all its related turbulence.

It is quite possible that without these events there would have been no Canada-U.S. Free Trade Agreement and no Europe 1992.

The will to press forward with them was never likely to originate in the parochial minds of politicians. It had to find its way into the minds of people and businesses first. The knowledge-based transformation of industry and its globalization imperative are what put it there. It follows that a Canada-U.S. trade marriage was never likely to occur other than in a time of significant economic turbulence and challenge. Making it work is going to take much more than being nice to one another. Empathy and courtesy, while desirable, are not going to be enough. The Canada-U.S. relationship has to be built on principles that will help each country to handle the external challenge better. These principles involve looking outward to competitiveness rather than inward to protectionism. Enhancing productivity needs to take precedence over Fortress North America. Not all industries are going to be global, of course; some will never evolve beyond regional status. There is nothing inevitable about globalization, except in the knowledge and information industries. These cannot help but be global. They are also the fastest-growing sectors. With all the impressive advances over the last decade in the development, storage, transmission and display of information, these technologies are still in their infancy and are poised for a major explosion.

Canada and the United States are major markets for one another's goods and services. Ontario, Canada's most populous province, ships close to 90 percent of all its exports to the United States. The United States, in turn, exports more to Ontario than it does to Japan. The Free Trade Agreement will enhance two-way trade even more. But the challenge from Japan and Europe is not going to diminish. Without appropriate responses from Canada and the United States, Japan's share of the North American market will increase. North America's response needs to emphasize improvements in quality, productivity, service and innovation. The parent-child model that has characterized U.S.-Canada business relations in the past has outlived its usefulness. Protected subsidiaries will never survive the external challenge. The language of parent-subsidiary relations has to go. Subsidiaries have to become affiliates or die under the smothering wing of paternalism. Both countries have to take more seriously their overall approach to knowledge and information. Furthermore, action is needed now. The future has arrived. Firms in both countries feel it. By the fall of 1989, less than one year after the signing of the Free Trade Agreement, Canadian authorities had received some 2,000 requests to have tariffs reduced more quickly. U.S. authorities had received 2,200 similar requests from firms and institutions in their country. People want to get on with it. They think that the free trade negotiators were too timid.

SPEEDING UP THE FREE TRADE ADJUSTMENT

In chapter 2 the point was made that some industries would need time to adjust to the dismantling of tariffs, and so the negotiators consulted with various industries and worked out an appropriate period of adjustment. The choices were ten years, five years or immediate. Given the thoroughness of consultation, why did both countries face within one year so many requests to speed up the process? Part of the reason is obvious. Some industries ended up in the ten-year process because there was a strong difference of opinion between the U.S. and Canadian sides. In pulp and paper and in steel, for example, the Canadians would have pressed for a short adjustment and the Americans for a longer one. In major appliances and machinery it would have been the other way around. Some of the requests to speed things up may have come from the Canadian pulp and paper industry and the American appliance industry. In other words, the requests may not match and may not be acted upon. Some requests, however, may have come from segments of an industry; for example, paint is part of the chemical industry, but its market is quite separate from that of other chemical products. If paint producers on both sides wanted to lower tariffs faster, that might be able to be done while the rest of the chemical industry remained on the schedule it has agreed to.

The sheer number of requests to accelerate the transition has, however, surprised officials on both sides. Business seems to be thinking differently about the opportunities under free trade after the agreement than before. It is not difficult to see why, especially from a Canadian perspective. Once the agreement was signed, it became clear that Canadian firms had to achieve U.S. levels of productivity or face loss of market share at home. For most, the best way to improve productivity was to specialize production and compete in the entire North American market. That is a considerable challenge for Canadian subsidiaries with U.S. parents, as we have discussed. For independent Canadian firms, it is more difficult still. How can a Canadian firm specialize before it has a share of the U.S. market to supply? How can it obtain a share of the U.S. market unless it specializes and gets its costs down? It is a catch-22 situation. When Australia and New Zealand signed a free trade accord in 1983, there followed a flurry of mergers and cross-ownership arrangements that facilitated specialization. Often the imperatives of marketing require a full product line, while the imperatives of production require a narrow product line. The cross-ownership arrangement allowed New Zealand firms to specialize their production and export to Australia while importing the rest of the product line from a trusted Australian source. Canadian firms, likewise, are having to position themselves in the American market in order to stand any chance of defending their home base. Alliances, mergers and acquisitions are all likely to be used. Furthermore, Canadian firms, which have not historically been as committed as U.S. firms to R & D and product innovation, are looking for some quick way to develop differentiated products with which to enter the U.S. market. Those without the in-house skills are seeking alliances in Europe and the Far East because they have to move quickly.

The result of all this is that once Canadian firms have faced up to what they have to do to survive under free trade, the remaining tariffs become an impediment in the transition. Component parts imported from the United States cost more because of the tariff and raise Canadian production costs, and exports to the United States face a tariff as well. Under free trade it is products rather than technology that cross borders. The volume of product trade rises sharply, and the tariff barriers, even though they are declining, become more of a nuisance. Firms want them eliminated. This is equally true for Canadian subsidiaries of U.S. parents. While specialization for them is easier because of corporate affiliation, once it is achieved, the level of north-south trade increases sharply, and the remaining tariffs become an impediment to the needed transition. These thousands of requests to speed up the Free Trade Agreement may be signalling that firms one way or another want to get on with the transition, and that the time schedule designed to insulate them from sudden pain has turned into an impediment. To the extent that this is true, it is a healthy sign.

PARENTS AND SUBSIDIARIES

The words parent and subsidiary evoke a nurturing, caring relationship flowing primarily from the parent. Subsidiaries traditionally leaned on their parents for technology and management skills. They built up over time enough in-house competence to learn fast and to adapt but not to innovate. As a result, many subsidiaries do not have the capacity in-house to survive the globalization of competition without parent help. In chapter 5 a number of suggestions were made to subsidiary managers about the kinds of initiatives they need to take to manage the transition successfully. Those suggestions stem from the clear realization that the status quo will not do. Subsidiaries cannot survive without fundamental strategic change. The sad truth is that their parents can no longer protect them from global competition. The parents are under attack themselves. The Free Trade Agreement provides both an opportunity and an impetus for change in parent-subsidiary relations. Since American subsidiaries in Canada account for such a large percentage of Canada's economic activity, it matters to Canadians how the change in parent-subsidiary structure is handled.

It matters to Americans too, but for a different reason. The American perspective is that the result has to achieve greater overall efficiency. The American focus is on global competition with Japan and Europe. The Canadian focus is on what role the subsidiary will end up with. Will it become a marketing center with all its production shifted to American parent facilities? Will it become an integrated factory subordinated to parent-company direction? Or will it evolve with a more attractive and responsible role in the corporation's overall global strategy? It is hard to say in general terms. The subsidiary's role will depend on industry conditions, subsidiary depth and competence and parent attitudes: industry conditions because globalization hits some industries harder than others; subsidiary competence because the more attractive and responsible roles require a lot of it; and parent attitude because some corporate cultures can handle the "not invented here" syndrome better than others and can therefore tolerate more subsidiary initiative.

Becoming Internationally Competitive

One increasingly popular approach taken by large companies facing global competition is to create an essentially competitive environment within the company. The way this works is that most products are manufactured in more than one location (smaller plants are often seen as easier to manage efficiently than very large ones). The company then encourages international competition between plants making the same product. Encouragement takes the form of sharing cost-performance data and assigning to the most efficient plant the ongoing technical support and product-renewal role. The high-cost plant becomes the swing plant for fluctuations in demand. Corporate units throughout the world compete for preeminence within the corporation. Those that fall behind get shut down. The corporate culture shifts from parental to competitive. Instead of a parent-subsidiary culture, it is more like an affiliation of equals. The head office may be a little more equal than others, but all affiliates have to justify their existence and take more of their destiny into their own hands. In these competitive corporate environments there are no handouts, and there is no protection. Subsidiaries become affiliates. They no longer copy their parents, and they no longer get babied. The familiar picture of the duck leading all its baby ducklings in a row to water no longer symbolizes the mature relationship between parent and affiliates. The mature relationship is driven by the very real external pressures of global competition. It is these pressures that are responsible for the transformation of subsidiaries to affiliates. Those subsidiaries that cannot make the transformation and supply some of the initiative will have to settle for lesser roles such as marketing centers or integrated suppliers.

Retaining the Capacity to Adapt

In turbulent times the capacity to adapt is very valuable. One of the great benefits of being international is that the firm is bombarded with market stimuli from all over the world. Information about technology, consumer tastes and product trends will vary from country to country, and in the variances can be found information of great value. Of course, the firm has to have high-caliber people in its international affiliates to pick up, distill and communicate the important stimuli. It also has to have a culture that listens. Many international firms are geared up for one-way communication from the head office. Learning from their affiliates does not come easily. There is evidence that Japanese businesses are more accustomed to learning. Many Japanese businessmen visited North America in the late seventies and early eighties to look at factories, distribution channels and product designs. Not only were they paying attention, their companies were too. Judging by the flow of well-designed products that later hit the shores of North America from Japan, Japanese firms were accustomed to listening and learning. Somehow, in North America listening and learning are not high among our institutional achievements. When an American goes abroad, there is customarily no great corporate curiosity about what he or she learned. The North American focus on quick results has relegated learning to an individual function, and individuals are not all that loyal to their employers in the era of mergers and acquisitions.

The ability of Japanese firms to learn better permits them to adapt their products faster to the real needs of consumers around the world. Part of the learning challenge is to have able people in key affiliates around the world who know what they are looking for and have the channels through which to communicate it and the credibility to be heard. But good people will not stay long in affiliates that do not have an interesting role or mandate. Emasculate your subsidiaries in the name of global efficiency, and you lose the opportunity to learn from them. Transform them into contributing affiliates, and they can teach you if you let them. In the grounds of Cypress Gardens in Florida stands a banyan tree noted for its age and size. Branches have spread out from the central trunk thirty to forty yards in all directions. At periodic intervals the major branches have dropped roots to the ground. The roots have taken hold, thickened and become like tributary trunks supporting and feeding the growing branches. Without those tributary trunks the central trunk could never support such far-flung branches. Successful international firms have to put roots down in key market areas in order to retain the capacity to learn from those areas. Roots, in this sense, refer to mandates of significance, and mandates as discussed in chapter 5 have to be earned by initiative and research efforts in the affiliate. The head office needs to reward and encourage such affiliate initiative: in other words, drop roots down and see if they take hold.

Roots in Canada

As a general rule, writers about globalization urge businesses to establish operations in the three major markets of the world: Europe, Japan and North America. The view is that it is difficult to be a global competitor without a significant presence in these "triad" markets. While authors may argue whether a particular industry is global or regional, or whether regional is just a step toward global, they do not usually argue whether Canada should be regarded as a triad nation. Their attention is clearly on Europe and Japan. In the analogy of the banyan tree, corporate roots should be set down in the major markets of the world, and Canada clearly does not qualify. But this constitutes a dilemma for many large American firms. Their operations in Canada are in fact much bigger and more profitable than their operations in Europe and Japan. Take GE as an example. Its traditional focus has been on North and South America; it has never been a significant force in Europe or Japan; and it has always had a broad multidivisional focus. GE in 1989 was in the process of trying to alter both its product and its market focus. It aimed to be either number one or number two in the world in each of the product areas it competed in, and it aimed to compete worldwide. However, because it was not organizationally strong in Europe and Japan, GE was trying to form international alliances in these countries. Its Canadian organization, which was strong managerially and technically, was looking for a role in the new strategy. Alliances are not like subsidiaries. They are not as easy to fold into a global strategy, and sometimes they are not as easy to learn from.

Many large American companies, therefore, face the presence of a significant resource in Canada along with a significant challenge elsewhere. The Canadian resource, furthermore, is undergoing major transition because of the Free Trade Agreement. It is emerging from a generalist strategy in a protected environment to a focussed strategy in a competitive environment. It is moving from subsidiary to affiliate. The question for American executives is whether the Canadian resource can be utilized in their global quest. Already a number of possible roles have emerged for the Canadian affiliate. These include the following:

1. Handling small overseas orders that require adaptation
2. Managing corporate assets in noncore regions such as Latin America, Africa, Eastern Europe and so on
3. Producing small-volume products
4. Doing design and engineering projects for the corporation as a whole

With the exception of role 2, there is not much future in these roles. Some of the emerging nations may well take their place among the world leaders in time, so there is hope in the second role, but it is a future hope. The roles are based largely on Canada's experience with small-volume activity and its sensitivity to emerging nations. They represent an attempt to tap the strengths built up by Canadian subsidiaries under protectionism. They are not all that forward looking. If Canadian subsidiaries make the transition to competing affiliates successfully, they will begin to lose their distinctive skills in small-volume activity. Successful Canadian affiliates will want to play a role in the overall global strategy of their corporations. What are the prospects for such a role? Will corporate cultures allow affiliates to play a core role in their global activity? The answer, of course, will vary, but many firms have already signalled that it will be positive if affiliates earn their way. By establishing a competitive internal environment, they have set the ground rules for global participation. If the Canadian affiliate becomes the low-cost supplier or the technological leader in a particular product area, it earns global responsibility. In this sense the affiliate becomes more like a product division than a subsidiary. This is the nature of the change required in Canada, and it is the reason why Canadian affiliates have to become well plugged in to overall corporate activity.

While the Canadian affiliate lacks the market glamour of Europe or Japan, it often represents a significant resource that can help the corporation in its global quest. The era of parental nurturing of subsidiaries is over. But if the subsidiary can transform itself into a competing affiliate, it should be rewarded with global responsibility in its areas of strength. If it cannot make the transformation, it may have to settle for a less strategic and more compliant role. In this event it may lose most of its good people over time, and with them the ability to learn from and adapt to the Canadian market. The Free Trade Agreement has, after all, been built on the principle of two markets under the national-treatment principle. There remains a very real risk that those American companies that end up with strategically dependent Canadian operations will lose market share in Canada.

UNSETTLED ISSUES FROM THE FREE TRADE AGREEMENT

Now that the Free Trade Agreement has been signed, political attention has moved on to other matters, as it always does. Left behind to tidy up in quiet anonymity are the lesser-known lights who traditionally do all the real work. The negotiators of the agreement were unable to agree in a number of important areas and therefore established joint committees to try to sort out some complex issues over a longer time period. The committees meet under the umbrella of the Canada-U.S. Trade Commission, co-chaired by John Crosbie and Carla Hills. Special committees are in place on auto trade, faster implementation, harmonization of technical barriers, government procurement and export subsidies. The issue of faster implementation has already been addressed in this chapter, and the committee working on it may well be ready to recommend some acceleration of the tariff schedule in the near future if the concerns of smaller firms can be handled. The auto-trade panel is in place because auto trade represents such a major proportion of Canada-U.S. trade, and the United States has a large auto-trade deficit—although not primarily with Canada. American automotive producers are concerned about the increasing level of Japanese investment in Canada to produce cars for the U.S. market. They would like to see the local-content rule changed from 50 percent to 60 percent for the automotive sector. If this were accepted, Japanese cars made in Canada would require 60 percent North American content in order to qualify for duty-free entry into the U.S. market. This issue was unresolved, and the 50 percent local-content rule written in the agreement still prevailed.

Export Subsidies

That the free trade negotiators could not agree on the subsidy question should have come as no surprise. Earlier chapters have alluded to its complexity. The challenge facing the committee now is to reduce the uncertainty in trade by defining more clearly what constitutes a subsidy. The committee got under way in 1989 on its five-to-seven-year task. Helpfully, the GATT in Geneva also had a group working on subsidies, so there was an opportunity for synergy. However, the committee's task promises to be an awkward one. Americans think that Canada is the chief offender when it comes to subsidies, and Canadians think that it is the United States, specifically at the state level. While there is evidence of subsidies on both sides, the question of whether a subsidy is an export subsidy is also an issue. Canada exports over three times more as a percent of gross national product (GNP) than does the United States. Because of Canada's greater trade intensity, a subsidy in Canada is intrinsically more likely to affect exports than a similar subsidy in the United States.

It is going to be difficult to find a fair resolution of the subsidy issue, but it is important nonetheless. If definitions prove elusive, another approach is to limit the scale of subsidies. For example, a foreign investor looking to build a plant in either Vermont or Canada's Maritimes could easily face government subsidy competition unless the subsidy agreement specified a limit. In this case subsidy limits would reduce the incidence of foolish government expenditures spurred on by competing for investment. The chief hope, however, is still for some agreement on the definition of a subsidy, hopefully in harmony with the GATT's deliberations. The discussions are going to be sensitive and complex, not the kind that respond to preposterous opening positions and combative, push-in-the-bayonet-until-you-hit-backbone negotiation tactics. Both sides are in for the long haul, and a degree of patience and honesty and the dexterity associated with a mature relationship are needed.

While these discussions are going on, the binational panel will be announcing decisions on specific cases referred to it. From these decisions will accrue a set of precedents that may help the committee in its deliberations. The softwood lumber dispute between Canada and the United States went on for seven years, which is far too long for business. The binational panel will streamline dispute resolution as well as contribute to a better understanding of what a subsidy is.

Harmonization of Technical Barriers

Are American electric ranges really unsafely wired, or are Canadian wiring standards really a trade impediment? Are Canadian fire-retardant cedar shingles really a fire hazard, or are the regulations of Los Angeles really a trade impediment? The Free Trade Agreement does not itself call for harmonization of standards and regulations, so the harmonization committees can reasonably agree to disagree. But if they did so unnecessarily, that would be a shame. North America is under competitive attack, and unnecessary waste should be eliminated wherever possible. A number of cost-saving trade-offs should be undertaken to simplify and facilitate trade between the two countries. Part of the idea of the Free Trade Agreement was that both Canada and the United States would benefit at the expense of third countries. If more benefit can be derived from eliminating unnecessary technical trade barriers, they ought to be eliminated. There is no point in shooting ourselves in the foot.

At the same time some trade impediments may be more difficult to deal with. In 1989 a GATT ruling was issued against Canada for restricting imports of American ice cream and yogurt. The reason for Canada's restrictions was that Canadian ice-cream and yogurt producers had to pay more for milk and therefore could not compete with American producers. The reason they had to pay more for milk was that Canada regulated the supply and price of milk through its milk-marketing boards. This kind of direct regulation almost always results in higher-than-world prices. However, it also puts more money into the hands of dairy farmers and gives them collective power in relation to large supermarkets. The problem is that if American imports of ice cream and yogurt cannot be restricted, then the marketing board loses its monopoly control over price and supply. The cost of direct regulation in a protected economy is higher prices, a cost Canada was more or less willing to bear. But under free trade the cost of direct regulation is loss of market share, and that is more serious. Canada has a number of direct agricultural marketing boards with power over price and supply. The Free Trade Agreement does not prohibit them, but international competition itself will probably finish them off. The GATT ruling virtually made direct regulation of price and supply untenable. Canada's marketing boards face an unpromising future; their role may have to be limited simply to marketing.

While the social challenge of reorienting Canada's marketing boards may take some time, there is no reason for other forms of regulatory harmonization to be delayed. In many areas the differences between Canadian and American regulations are just not substantive. In other areas one approach is manifestly better than the other. The absence of pressure from the Free Trade Agreement is probably a good thing. There is enough pressure from global competition. Regulatory harmonization is an area where Canada and the United States can readily agree to disagree but should not unless the reasons are substantial.

Government Procurement

The term government procurement has a slightly obscene ring to it. It is used frequently in contract language to reflect government's role as a buyer. Government buys a lot from business and has long since developed buying policies with a political twist to them. Usually the political twist is to favor local firms over firms from other states and national firms rather than foreign firms. In other words, the politics in government procurement inhibits trade by favoring local suppliers. Americans are encouraged to "buy American." Canadian federal and provincial governments have used their buying power to help small firms get started and to stimulate innovation.

When the Free Trade Agreement was negotiated, there was much discussion about loosening government procurement policies on both sides of the border to permit Canadians to bid as equals on American government contracts and to permit Americans to do likewise in Canada. Both governments, however, got concerned enough that the final agreement contained only minor revisions to existing arrangements. "Ground breaking but not earth moving" was how one Canadian official described the result. A committee is now in place to try to expand on the government procurement clause of the agreement. So it should be. It would be just like politicians to urge the benefits of competition on everyone else but to resist it on themselves. In a more serious vein, one of the benefits of international agreements on trade is that they can sometimes stop government inefficiency that is otherwise difficult to stop in democratic societies. The issue of competitive subsidies is a case in point. States may try to outbid one another to attract foreign investment unless there is a lid on how high the subsidies can go. The lid may not be popular, but without it a destructive subsidy war, from which only the foreign investor benefits, is difficult to stop. Constraining government procurement policy through the Free Trade Agreement could have a similar benefit. Governments may simply have to buy more competitively. That is not a bad result. It will take some getting used to: the pork barrel will have less in it. International agreements like the Canada-U.S. Free Trade Agreement can do a lot to save governments from foolish policies they might otherwise have difficulty avoiding. The government procurement section of the agreement will do more than any other to drive this message home, and so one hopes that the committee working on it will be able to reach a broader consensus that politicians will accept.

Other Committees

There are also committees working on intellectual property—patent and copyright laws—and trade in services. These are both difficult but important areas. In the area of intellectual property there is a GATT committee hard at work that may provide helpful leadership, but in services the Canada-U.S. committee is leading the way. The committee expects to draft rules on an industry-by-industry basis within the service sector and use them to initiate

GATT discussion at the forthcoming Uruguay round. This is a ground-breaking challenge, and an important one to the United States, but it is going to take a lot of creativity to get an earth-moving result. The chances of a closer Canada-U.S. alliance on services are undoubtedly better than the chances for a GATT agreement. However, if Canada and the United States can agree on some rules for trade in services, U.S. officials could immediately go to work to secure the agreement of Europe and Japan to them. Liberalizing trade in services among the major economic regions of the world would be a significant achievement.

There are two obsessions that, while not the subject of special committees, could still be troublesome to the full implementation of free trade. One is the American obsession with security and the other the Canadian obsession with culture. The American obsession with national security puzzles Canadians. Not only are we in the era of *glasnost*, we are also in the era of globalization, and Canadians are often surprised at the level of American resentment over foreign investment and the frequent use of national-security concerns as an explanation. The 1989 takeover of Columbia Pictures by Sony was a recent example. Many Americans expressed concern that Sony would transform Columbia into a Japanese propaganda organ. Given the scale of American investment in Canada, Canadians get worried when they see such defensive reactions to foreign investment in the United States.

Canada's obsession with culture puzzles Americans. They do not know what Canadians are worried about. When Canadians try to explain the problems of living next door to a giant and striving to retain cultural independence, they are usually greeted with a yawn. When they go further and talk about how difficult it is for Canadian cultural industries—for example, broadcasting and book and magazine publishing—to compete with American firms who write off their creative costs against the U.S. market and serve Canada on a marginal overflow basis, the argument starts to sound like protectionism to Americans. Why don't Canadian cultural industries compete internationally, they wonder? Many Canadians wonder that too. However, the cultural industries were exempted from the Free Trade Agreement. The danger is that Canada will use that exemption to impede trade unnecessarily.

WHERE ARE WE HEADED?

Nothing was more symbolic of the power of globalization to break down barriers than the destruction of the Berlin Wall. The sight of people dancing on the wall and of heavy equipment beginning to demolish parts of it stirred the soul. Soviet leaders applauded the decision. The West was ecstatic. The cold-war isolation was over. The decade of the nineties began full of promise. Globalization was king and national governments were in retreat. Part of the appeal of the globalization phenomenon was its liberating power, but another part was its ability to redress global wealth disparities, which strong national governments have tended to perpetuate. But where is globalization leading us? How will it change North American society?

Diagnosing the future can be a risky business. Not many people are good at discerning megatrends. The dramatic changes in the Soviet Union and Eastern Europe have taken most people by surprise. Writing about where we are headed is therefore intimidating. As a result, these next few pages will focus on two aspects of the future that are already becoming clear. They offer no crystal ball, no vision 2000, just a few thoughts about living in a society committed to competing and to learning.

A Society Committed to Competing

The United States and Canada have been the wealthiest nations in the world for several decades. It is always disquieting to see other nations catching up with one's own achievements, and it is even more disquieting to lose the number one spot in world economic leadership. This is how globalization is affecting the United States. In the post–World War II era American policy had as its primary objective the rebuilding of the shattered economies of Europe and Japan. With visionary foresight American policymakers argued that a strong and independent Europe and Japan were in the best long-term interest of the United States. It should not come as any surprise, therefore, that these nations have now caught up. That was, after all, the policy objective. Single-handed U.S. economic leadership was a temporary necessity. Sharing economic power is a more desirable norm. Otherwise the cry of hegemony would be heard, and other nations would begin to distrust a global economic system with no room at the top and no major shifts in power.

It is, however, still difficult to lose the top spot in that one has to come face to face with the possibility that the way things have traditionally been done is not necessarily the best way. When competition really begins to bite, businesses and individuals look for new and better ways to do things. The result is a lot of turbulence and challenge. This is discomforting for many people. Success in an era of competition means working alongside people from other cultures. Businesses do this by forming alliances, but ultimately it is people who have to learn how to make them work. The opportunity and the challenge to learn are greater in a competitive than in a protected environment.

The task of making the economy more competitive involves restructuring business units and attitudes. In the United States, business restructuring is done by mergers and acquisitions. There have been many of them during the eighties, and increasingly they have involved foreign businesses. Not all of them have been helpful to the cause of improved efficiency, but many have. What is becoming increasingly clear, however, is that restructuring only presents an opportunity for improvement. Achieving international competitiveness is as much about the management of people as about the management of deals. Yet is is the deal makers that hit the headlines. When the fun and the spotlight of the megamerger poker game are over, product cost and product quality are the factors that really influence competitiveness, and these in turn involve the management of people. It is difficult, even with the levelest of playing fields, for an American firm with adversarial management-labor relations to compete with a Japanese firm whose workers routinely generate ideas about improving productivity and quality. The management of people is essential to the enhancement of competitiveness.

Canada's competitiveness challenge is different. Decades of economic protectionism left the country with a much more difficult restructuring problem than the United States. Canada's national policy was built on the theme of independence. High tariffs encouraged Canadian production for the Canadian market. There was no specialization or focus. Using largely imported technology, Canadian business produced multiple products for its own small market at relatively high cost. This was no way to create an internationally competitive economy, as many other nations who have tried the same thing can attest. Foreign ownership was extensive and innovation was not, and when a nation's economy is neither efficient nor innovative, it is difficult to compete. Canada has therefore rejected protectionism with its legacy of balkanization, state intervention and inward-looking adversarialism in favor of free trade and international competition.

The transition will be a difficult one for Canada. The challenge facing Canadian subsidiaries of U.S. parents is a microcosm of it. But while the Canadian challenge is a tougher one, Canadians may be more ready to tackle it. The 1988 Canadian election was fought over free trade, and Canadians decided to compete. Canada has never been a leading economic power in the world and hence is more ready to learn. Having rejected protectionism at home in favor of competition, Canada will oppose any American protectionist instincts as the trade dialogue between the two countries intensifies. One thing Canadians have learned is that protectionism for its own sake leaves a bitter legacy of inefficiency. There may well be need for reciprocity in world markets, and one may well have to play hardball to get it, but Canadians will try to prevent reciprocity from turning into managed, protected trade.

Ultimately, Canada, like all small nations, will be quite vulnerable under free trade. The restructuring of Canadian industry to a north-south rather than an east-west pattern will leave Canadian firms much more dependent on access to the American market than

American firms will be on access to the Canadian market. This vulnerability is shared by other nations like Sweden or Denmark. Once protectionism is discarded because of its inefficiencies, international competitiveness leaves the small nations ever more vulnerable to the fairness and openness of the world's major markets. As a result, Canada enters its free trade marriage with the United States as the more vulnerable partner. Nevertheless, it brings to the relationship a level of commitment that might be helpful to North America's chances in the globally competitive battles ahead.

One final word on global competition. It requires a society committed to efficiency and innovation. The pace of change will require adaptiveness and flexibility. New technologies have to be harnessed faster and used more intelligently. It is not a time for rigidity. It is not a time for security. It is an unpredictable, uncomfortable time filled with both challenge and opportunity. The impact on people in terms of new relationships, new career paths and new management systems will be staggering. But at least they will know that they have been hit by an external challenge. That is when people are at their best. Reliance on government will not help. Both the Canadian and American governments are wrestling with massive deficits as it is, but more to the point, under free trade governments are supposed to refrain from intervention. If there is pain to be felt—and there is pain in competitive societies—it has to be felt by businesses and individuals directly.

A Society Committed to Learning

Many factors point to the importance of learning as a major factor in the competitiveness battle. We are, after all, entering the knowledge era. Anything to do with the development, storage, transmission and display of information seems somehow to be a growth industry. Information technologies are ready to explode. Globalization itself is anchored in the knowledge industries. The critical competitive factor is the skill and training of people. The information technologies are changing the nature of work and the nature of education. In a time of rapid change, education and training must be ongoing. People must be able to update and upgrade themselves several times during their working lives. There is a massive challenge to North America in these facts.

Learning has been relegated to a secondary activity in North America for decades. It is almost as though economic leadership blunted the urge to learn. American management techniques were eagerly disseminated throughout Europe and Japan during the sixties and seventies. Now it is Japanese management that has captured the world stage. It is North America's turn to learn, but its schools have slipped into mediocrity and decline. Teachers are not respected in American society the way they are in Europe and Japan. Academics seldom find their way into corporate board-rooms the way they do in Europe and Japan. Businesses are not organized to learn. Japanese managers on assignment in North America will go to great lengths to see that their children get educated in Japan, even if it means that the mother takes them there before their assignment is over. The fear is that if they leave education too long, their children will never catch up. They have a deep dedication and commitment to learning that is lacking in North America. This gives them a competitive edge that is genuinely hard to match, especially in knowledge-based industries.

Globalization is forcing North America to face up to its learning deficiency. International comparisons of educational achievement have become commonplace even though embarrassing. On the bright side, technology is also transforming the learning process, customizing it, speeding it up and making the conventional class-room increasingly obsolete. The institutional barriers to improved education and training, which might otherwise be powerful, are being mitigated by technology.

Technology, however, cannot put the desire to learn into students. That has to come from families or from society as a whole, and both have been failing. The dedication of parents to the training of their children has been diminished by dual-career pressures. Furthermore, the standards of society have been al-lowed to slip. Drugs impede learning. Pornography impedes learning. We are making ourselves uncompetitive in the name of freedom. Profanity parades as vocabulary. There is not much reinforcement in society for those dedicated to learning. Somehow we have to raise our social standards again and provide an environment as conducive to learning as that in Europe or Japan. Less parochial and more outward-looking media would help too. North Americans need to know more about other parts of the world if it is necessary to compete with them. Two trips to China do not make an expert.

Institutions can learn as well as individuals. Information can be organized and stored electronically in imaginative ways. Businesses are going to have to learn how to learn from their people in spite of the lack of corporate loyalty that will result from the trauma of restructuring—or perhaps because of it. Access to relevant timely information and speed in utilizing it commercially will become increasingly important for success in global competition. Learning is going to matter more and more.

What about the Disadvantaged?

Many Canadians who voted for free trade because of the globalization of competition had some serious reservations about the level of caring and compassion possible in a truly competitive society. What about the disadvantaged in such a society? What about the number of suicides among Japanese students? Many church leaders in Canada opposed free trade on compassionate grounds. They saw the prospect of a society so bent on efficiency and competition that there would be no place in it for the learning-disabled. Society from this perspective is about to become polarized between the rich and well-informed and the poor and ignorant. As information technology leaps ahead, the level of personal investment in time and training required to participate in it will climb too. It will become increasingly difficult for those left behind to catch up. What we are in danger of doing with our information technology is creating a society in which not everyone can participate. Technology will outstrip the ability of many to understand and adapt.

This is a very plausible view, but one that personally I do not
ntirely accept. The danger is clear, but the inevitability is not. The
iew would be more persuasive if our social standards and educa-
ional institutions had been improving steadily over the last decade
ather than getting worse. An alternative view would be that North
Americans need a challenge to capture the imagination of their
outh and catapult them to higher personal and educational stand-
rds. There is every possibility that globalization could be that
hallenge. Furthermore, there is every possibility that information
echnology will help the learning-disabled to learn faster. What
ociety should ensure is ongoing public access to its education and
nformation systems regardless of age. The essential choice we
ace is whether we should try to leave our children a legacy of
rotection, safety and security or a legacy of competition, chal-
enge and risk. The former may make us feel better, but the latter
vould be better for them. One thing is clear. The moral high ground
s not at either extreme. It is somewhere in between. Globally it
nay be much closer to the competition ethic than people have been
villing to acknowledge.

CONCLUSION

The 1980s came to a close with a breathtaking series of events
n Eastern Europe that transformed the political landscape away
rom its traditional preoccupations. These events will exert a
)owerful influence on the politics of the nineties. Marxism and
evolutionary socialism are in retreat. Their ability to help mankind
ias been shown to be deficient in an unmistakable way. The
nessage has surged through many of the less developed countries.
New economic policies loosening the role of government and
ncouraging independent enterprise are increasingly common.

Next to these stirring world events, the Canada-U.S. Free Trade
Agreement seems an almost timid contribution to the mood of our
ime. Nevertheless, for Canada it was a transforming event of great
iignificance. The need for change in the Soviet Union, Eastern
Europe and the less developed world was more pronounced. Their

policies had led to economic stagnation and decline for decades as well as stringent limits on personal freedom. So while the courage of leaders in these countries to address change is to be applauded, still the need was clear and the cost of not changing high. The Canada-U.S. Free Trade Agreement, by comparison, was a move in harmony with the main thrust of existing policy to accommodate the globalization of competition. For the United States, the agreement was not a high-profile public issue and did not require any gut-wrenching political decisions. However, encouraged by the boldness of world events, the United States signed a framework agreement in late 1989 to move toward free trade with Mexico. In normal times the prospects of anything substantive coming out of a framework agreement between two such different countries would not be promising. But these are not normal times. Change beyond the most optimistic imagination is engulfing the world. The cobwebs of divisive nationalism are being swept away. The unthinkable has become possible. A free trade area for all of North America is not out of the question.

At the same time we should not in our euphoria do a shabby job of implementing the Canada-U.S. Free Trade Agreement. We have to pay attention to details and to different national aspirations and challenges. This book was written in part to draw attention to the different perspectives of Canada and the United States in entering the agreement, and to point out how the agreement differs from Europe 1992 and what some of the implications are for business. The intent was to promote understanding and get the marriage off to a good start. It would be a shame to get bogged down in the details of implementation at a time when the rest of the world is acting with such boldness.

There is a need for much goodwill between Canada and the United States during the nineties. The Free Trade Agreement has shifted the relationship to a more mature level with more common objectives. The adversarial negotiating style of the past has to go. We are in this relationship for the long term. We need to understand one another better and, judging from the *Maclean's* survey in appendix A, we have a long way to go. Fortunately, the nineties

vill be a time of sweeping global transformation calling for
ncreased understanding worldwide. What a great time to be alive!
The learning that comes from the challenge of Canada-U.S. free
rade cannot help but make it easier for both countries to deal with
he exhilarating changes occurring elsewhere in the world. Indeed,
f the pace of change witnessed in the last two years of the eighties
ontinues through the decade of the nineties, we could be headed
or a dramatically different new millennium than anyone supposed.

APPENDIX A:
MACLEAN'S/DECIMA POLL

A NORTH-SOUTH DIALOGUE

The complete Maclean's poll of 1,000 Canadians and 1,000 Americans was conducted by Toronto-based Decima Research. The results are considered accurate to within 3.3 percentage points 19 times out of 20:

(To Canadians) What is the most important problem facing Canada today, the one that concerns you the most?
Pollution/environment 17%
Unemployment 10%
Free trade 9%
Deficit/national debt 9%
Social/moral 9%
Inflation 5%

(To Americans) What is the most important problem facing the United States today, the one that concerns you the most?
Drugs/alcohol 18%
Deficit 16%
Social/moral 6%
Homeless/poverty 6%
Pollution/environment 5%
Economy 5%

Would you be prepared to see either taxes increased significantly or services cut in order to reduce the federal deficit?

	Canada	United States
Yes	48%	54%
No	49%	44%

Do you feel that you can count on business to act in the public interest all of the time, most of the time, hardly ever or never?

	Canada	United States
Never	8%	7%
Hardly ever	38%	37%
Most of the time	48%	54%
All of the time	5%	3%
No opinion	1%	

Do you feel that you can count on government to act in the public interest all of the time, most of the time, hardly ever or never?

	Canada	United States
Never	8%	5%
Hardly ever	36%	32%
Most of the time	51%	60%
All of the time	5%	3%
No opinion	1%	

In time of crisis, do you believe government should or should not have the power to declare a national emergency and remove all civil rights?

	Canada	United States
Should not	49%	56%
Should	48%	41%
No opinion	3%	3%

Do you view the following as an absolute right that can never be taken away, or as a limited right, one which in certain circumstances can be limited by government?

a) Job protection for a woman on pregnancy leave

	Canada	United States
Limited right	29%	27%
Absolute right	71%	72%
No opinion		1%

b) A publicly funded health care system available to all, regardless of financial situation

	Canada	United States
Limited right	29%	46%
Absolute right	71%	52%
No opinion		3%

c) A guaranteed minimum income for everyone

	Canada	United States
Limited right	37%	47%
Absolute right	62%	51%
No opinion	1%	2%

d) Child care available to everyone who wants it

	Canada	United States
Limited right	50%	53%
Absolute right	50%	46%
No opinion		1%

Have you ever been robbed or assaulted?

	Canada	United States
Yes	21%	26%
No	79%	74%

Do you own a handgun?

	Canada	United States
Yes	3%	24%
No	97%	75%
No opinion		1%

Are you afraid to walk alone on the streets of your community at night?

	Canada	United States
Yes	24%	31%
No	76%	69%

Young Americans between the ages of 18 and 24 expressed greater fear of walking alone at night in their communities than did Canadians of the same age group.
Canadian average	24%
Canadians (18 to 24)	18%
U.S. Average	31%
Americans (18 to 24)	38%

Have you ever used illegal drugs?

	Canada	United States
Yes	11%	13%
No	89%	86%
No opinion		1%

> Young Americans are more likely than young Canadians to have used illegal drugs.
> | | |
> |---|---|
> | Canadian average | 11% |
> | Canadians (18 to 24) | 17% |
> | U.S. Average | 13% |
> | Americans (18 to 24) | 31% |

Would you favor or oppose shutting down a major company that provided many jobs in your community if it was polluting the environment?

	Canada	United States
Oppose	37%	33%
Favor	60%	64%
No opinion	3%	3%

What do you think is better for Canada/the United States: that new immigrants be encouraged to maintain their distinct culture and ways, or to change their distinct culture and ways to blend with the larger society?

	Canada	United States
Maintain	34%	47%
Change	61%	51%
No opinion	5%	2%

> Young Canadians are more likely than young Americans to say that immigrants should change their customs.
> | | |
> |---|---|
> | Canadian average | 61% |
> | Canadians (18 to 24) | 57% |
> | U.S. average | 51% |
> | Americans (18 to 24) | 34% |

Would you be happy, indifferent or unhappy if one of your children married someone from a different racial background?

	Canada	United States
Unhappy	13%	32%
Indifferent	60%	51%
Happy	25%	15%
No opinion	2%	2%

Have you ever been the victim of racial or ethnic discrimination?

	Canada	United States
Yes	12%	18%
No	89%	82%

(To Canadians) If you had to describe Americans in one word, what would it be?

Snobs	11%
Good	9%
Friendly	8%
Pigheaded	6%
Aggressive	5%
Powerful	5%
Obnoxious	4%
Indifferent	4%
Stupid	3%
Rich	3%
Neighbors	3%
Capitalistic	3%
Don't know	8%

(To Americans) If you had to describe Canadians in one word, what would it be?

Friendly	28%
Nice	9%
Neighbors	6%
Wonderful	5%
Similar	4%
Satisfied	3%
Normal	3%
Delightful	2%
Northerners	2%
French	2%
Don't know	11%

Would you describe Canadians and Americans as essentially the same, mainly the same but with some small differences, mainly different but with some small similarities, or essentially different?

	Canada	United States
Essentially the same	13%	18%
Mainly the same	43%	60%
Mainly different	24%	15%
Essentially different	19%	6%
No opinion		2%

Would you strongly support, support, oppose or strongly oppose Canada and the United States adopting common and identical policy on all matters relating to defence and foreign affairs?

	Canada	United States
Strongly oppose	24%	4%
Oppose	36%	19%
Support	33%	58%
Strongly support	5%	15%
No opinion	2%	3%

Would you strongly favor, favor, oppose or strongly oppose Canada becoming the 51st state of the United States with full congressional representation and rights of American citizenship?

	Canada	United States
Strongly oppose	54%	10%
Oppose	31%	22%
Favor	12%	54%
Strongly favor	2%	12%
No opinion	1%	3%

Would you strongly favor, favor, oppose or
strongly oppose Canada and the United States
adopting a common currency?

	Canada	United States
Strongly oppose	21%	4%
Oppose	28%	19%
Favor	40%	62%
Strongly favor	9%	12%
No opinion	2%	2%

Are you aware that Canada and the United
States recently signed a Free Trade Agreement?

	Canada	United States
Yes	97%	57%
No	3%	43%

(To Canadians) Which one of these words, in
your view, best describes the ideal Canadian?
Tolerant 38%
Independent-minded 27%
Peaceful 26%
Aggressive 3%
Clean 3%
Sexy 1%
No opinion 1%

(To Americans) Which one of these words, in
your view best describes the ideal American?
Independent-minded 52%
Tolerate 21%
Aggressive 12%
Peaceful 12%
Clean 3%
Sexy 1%
No opinion 1%

(To Canadians) If you had to rate American
men/women on a scale of 1 to 10 where 1 was
"very unattractive" and 10 was "very
attractive", how would you place them?
mean attractiveness rating: 6.17

(To Americans) if you had to rate Canadian
men/women on a scale of 1 to 10 where 1 was
"very unattractive" and 10 was "very
attractive", how would you place them?
mean attractiveness rating: 6.31

(To Canadians) Would you like to send your
children to the United States to attend
university or college?
Yes 41%
No 58%
No opinion 2%

(To Americans) Would you like to send your
children to Canada to attend university or
college?
Yes 58%
No 39%
No opinion 3%

(To Canadians) Who would you say is Canada's
biggest trading partner?
United States 83%
Japan 9%
China 1%
Europe 1%
No opinion 6%

(To Americans) Who would you say is the United
States biggest trading partner?
Japan 69%
Canada 12%
China 3%
U.K./Britain 2%
Soviet Union 2%
Germany 2%
No opinion 6%

(To Canadians) Would you like to live in the
United States?
Yes 27%
No 73%

(To Americans) Would you like to live in
Canada?
Yes 42%
No 56%
No opinion 2%

(To Canadians) What do you least like about
Americans?
Superior attitude 25%
Nothing 10%
Lack of knowledge about Canada 7%
Aggressive 5%
Crime/Violence 4%
Loud 3%
Selfish/greedy 3%
Military 3%
Racial discrimination 3%
Pushy 2%
Unfriendly/rude 2%
Don't know 12%

(To Americans) What do you like least about
Canadians?
Nothing 37%
Do not know Canadians 18%
Do no know about them 14%
French-speaking 6%
They think they are better 3%
Don't know 4%
Arrogant 2%

(To Canadians) Do you know who the vice-
president of the United States is?
Yes, Dan Quayle 35%
No 56%
Yes, other 8%
No opinion 1%

(To Americans) Do you know who the prime
minister of Canada is?
Yes, Brian Mulroney 11%
No 81%
Yes, other 8%

APPENDIX B: THE CANADA-U.S. FREE TRADE AGREEMENT SYNOPSIS

Part One: Objectives and Scope

Chapter One: Objectives and Scope

This Chapter sets the tone for the Agreement as a whole. The objectives make clear the extent to which the Canada-United States Trade Agreement moves beyond other free-trade agreements negotiated under the GATT. Four previous agreements are particularly relevant: the 1960 European Free-Trade Area; the 1965 UK-Ireland Free-Trade Agreement; the 1983 Australia-New Zealand Closer Economic Relations Agreement; and the 1985 United States-Israel Agreement.

The new Canada-United States Agreement is broader in scope as it provides for liberalization in all sectors of the economy, including agriculture. No other trade agreement includes binding commitments on trade in services, business travel or investment. No other agreement provides a basis for developing new rules to deal with subsidies, dumping and countervailing measures.

The Chapter begins with a declaration that the Agreement is consistent with Article XXIV of the GATT, the Article which provides the framework in international law for negotiating free-trade agreements. It sets out a legal statement of the basic principle underlying the Agreement as a whole: Canada and the United States will treat each other's goods, services, investment, suppliers and investors as they treat their own insofar as the matters covered by this Agreement are concerned. Individual parts and chapters work out this principle in detail. Chapter Five in Part Two, for example, establishes national treatment for trade in goods and chapters Six, Seven, and Eight all contain important amplifications of this principle. Similarly, the services and investment chapters begin with a statement of this principle and then develop how it will be applied.

The Agreement recognizes that it is based on the precedents and commitments between Canada and the United States established in other bilateral and multilateral agreements. For purposes of interpretation, it indicates that the provisions of this Agreement take precedence over all other agreements unless there is a specific provision to the contrary. For example, Article 908 states that the undertakings of the two governments under the *Agreement on an International Energy Program* take precedence over the provisions of this Agreement.

The wide scope of the Agreement is indicated from the outset in the agreed objectives. The Agreement will:

- eliminate barriers to trade in goods and services between the two countries;

- facilitate conditions of fair competition within the free-trade area;

- significantly expand liberalization of conditions for cross-border investment;

- establish effective procedures for the joint administration of the Agreement and the resolution of disputes; and

- lay the foundation for further bilateral and multilateral co-operation to expand and enhance the benefits of the Agreement.

The Agreement will specifically involve federal, state, and provincial measures. While the two federal governments are the Parties to the Agreement, the important role of the states and provinces is recognized, for instance, in the commitments on wine and spirits.

Chapter Two: Definitions

In this chapter, words critical to the application of the agreement as a whole are defined. For example, the word "measure" is

requently used in the Agreement. It is defined as any governmental
law, regulation, procedure, requirement or practice. In effect, the
rights and obligations of the two governments basically involve what
measures they can and cannot take and how they can take them.

Part Two:
Trade in Goods

Part Two contains chapters three through twelve dealing with
trade in goods. It builds on the GATT, its ancillary agreements as well
as other existing arrangements involving the two governments such as
the Harmonized Commodity Description and Coding System (the so-
called Harmonized System by which imports are classified for
purposes of assessing customs duties), the *Canada-United States
Automotive Products Trade Agreement* and the *Agreement on an
International Energy Program*.. Where both governments were
satisfied with existing arrangements, they are incorporated by refer-
ence into the Agreement. For example, the *GATT Code on Technical
Barriers to Trade* is the basis of Chapter Six and the provisions of
GATT Article XX (General Exceptions) form the basis of chapter
Twelve. In most instances, however, Canada and the United States
have entered into new obligations unique to the Free-Trade
Agreement.

Chapters Three through Six and Eleven and Twelve contain
provisions applicable to all trade in goods. The four sectoral chapters,
Seven for Agriculture, Eight for Wine and Distilled Spirits, Nine for
Energy and Ten for Automotive Products, address issues of particular
concern to those sectors.

Chapter Three: Rules of Origin for Goods

The Agreement will eliminate all tariffs on trade between
Canada and the United States by January 1, 1998. However, both
countries will continue to apply their existing tariffs to imports from
other countries. Rules of origin are, therefore, needed to define those
goods which are entitled to duty-free, or "free-trade area" treatment
when exported from one country to the other.

Since the Agreement is intended to benefit the producers of
both countries and generate employment and income for Canadians
and Americans, origin rules require that goods traded under the

Agreement be produced in either country or both. The origin rule: establish the general principle that goods that are wholly produced o obtained in either Canada or the United States or both will qualify fo area treatment. Goods incorporating offshore raw materials o components will also qualify for area treatment if they have bee» sufficiently changed either in Canada or the United States, or both, to be classified differently from the raw materials or components from which they are made. In certain cases, goods, in addition to being classified differently, will also need to incur a certain percentage o manufacturing cost in either or both countries, in most cases 50 percent. This is particularly important for assembly operations.

In practical terms, goods other than those which originate wholly in either Canada and/or the United States, will have to incorporate some significant Canadian or US content. For example goods imported in bulk from offshore and repackaged and labelled ir the United States would not qualify for area treatment, while a produc incorporating only some imported components in most instance: would. A bicycle, for example, using Canadian steel for its frame and assembled in Canada using imported wheels and gears would qualify a: a product of Canadian origin, if 50 percent of its manufacturing cost i: accounted for in Canada and/or the United States.

Apparel made from fabrics woven in Canada or the United States will qualify for duty-free treatment whereas apparel made from offshore fabrics will qualify for duty-free treatment only up to the following levels:

	Non-Woolen Apparel	Woolen Apparel
	(in million square yard equivalent)	
Imports from Canada	50	6
Imports from the United States	10.5	1.1

Above these levels, apparel made from offshore fabrics will be considered, for tariff purposes, as products of the country from which the fabrics were obtained. The levels established for imports from Canada are well above current trade levels. Canadian clothing manufacturers, including manufacturers of fine suits, coats, snowsuits and parkas, can, for all practical purposes, continue to buy their fabric from the most competitive suppliers around the world and still benefit from duty-free access to the United States. In addition, should their exports to the United States consume more than 56 million square yards of imported fabric, they will pay the US tariff but be able to benefit from the drawback of Canadian duties paid on such fabric (see chapter Four).

There is a similar quantitative limit governing duty-free exports to the United States of non-woolen fabrics or textile articles woven or knitted in Canada from yarn imported from a third country. Such exports, otherwise meeting the origin rules, will benefit from area treatment up to a maximum annual quantity. The level has initially been set at 30 million square yards for the first four years. The two governments will revisit this issue after January 1, 1991 to work out a mutually satisfactory revision of this arrangement.

Producers may consult chapter 3 to see whether their goods will qualify for area treatment. General rules and principles are set out in articles 301 to 303 and in the Interpretation to Annex 301.2. Definitions are set out in Article 304. Rules relating to specific goods, based on classification under the Harmonized System, are set out in Annex 301.2.

Chapter 3 makes it clear that goods further processed in a third country before being shipped to their final destination would not qualify for area treatment. For example, a shirt sewn in Mexico from cloth both cut in the U.S. and woven in the U.S. from U.S. fibres would qualify for favourable duty treatment upon importation into the United States, but would not qualify for area treatment upon importation into Canada.

The chapter contains safeguards to prevent circumvention of the rules as well as a process for consultation and revision to ensure that the rules of origin evolve to take account of changes in production processes.

Chapter Four: Border Measures

Key to any free-trade agreement, and required by the provisions of the GATT, is the elimination of duties and other restrictions on substantially all the trade between the parties. Implementation of the provisions of Chapter Four will achieve this requirement by providing for the removal of the tariff, tariff-related measures, quantitative restrictions and other restrictive measures applied at the border on or before January 1, 1998. This transition period is consistent with similar transition periods established in previous agreements. For example, the European Community initially provided a twelve-year period. The Tokyo Round tariff cuts were phased in over eight years.

Tariffs

The tariff has been an important but waning import policy instrument in Canada for many decades. More than 75 percent of Canada-United States trade now moves free of duty. This figure, however, fails to take account of the trade which could take place but for tariffs. High U.S. tariffs -- 15 percent and more on petro-chemicals, metal alloys, clothing and many other products -- continue to pose serious barriers to the U.S. market and prevent Canadian firms from achieving the economies of scale on which increased competitiveness and employment in Canadian industry depend. In addition to high tariffs, escalating tariffs on resource-based products discourage the development of more sophisticated manufacturing in Canada. While a 1.7 cent per kilo tariff on zinc ore may not impose a significant barrier, a 19 percent tariff on zinc alloy has effectively retarded the establishment of a zinc metal fabricating industry in Canada. Additionally, the existence of Canadian tariffs on imports from the United States is often costly to Canadian consumers and producers.

This chapter provides for the gradual elimination of all remaining tariffs. The cuts will begin January 1, 1989 and after that date, no existing tariff may be increased unless specifically provided elsewhere in the Agreement (for example, in chapter Eleven providing for temporary emergency safeguards). Tariffs will be eliminated by January 1, 1998 on the basis of three formulas:

- for those sectors ready to compete now, tariffs will be eliminated on the Agreement entering into force on January 1, 1989, for example:

computers and equipment	some pork
some unprocessed fish	fur & fur garments
leather	whiskey
unwrought aluminum	ferro alloys
yeast	animal feeds
vending machines and parts	needles
airbrakes for railroad cars	skis
skates	warranty repairs

some paper-making machinery   motorcycles

- for other sectors, tariffs will be eliminated in five equal steps, starting on January 1, 1989, for example:

subway cars
printed matter
paper and paper products
paints
explosives
aftermarket auto parts

chemicals including resins
(excluding drugs and
cosmetics)
furniture
hardwood plywood
most machinery

- all other tariffs will be eliminated in ten steps, most starting on January 1, 1989, for example:

most agricultural products
textiles and apparel
softwood plywood
railcars

steel
appliances
pleasure craft
tires

Annex 401 (published separately) sets out the schedule of tariff cuts for each product according to its classification in the Harmonized System. If both countries agree, the staging can be accelerated. Both the European Community and the European Free-Trade Association concluded after a few years that they would benefit from accelerated tariff elimination. Australia and New Zealand are currently discussing speeding up their tariff reductions.

In the case of certain specialty steel items currently subject to temporary emergency safeguards by the United States, tariff cuts will not begin until October 1, 1989, as required by U.S. law. Large telephone switching equipment will be phased out in three annual steps ending January 1, 1991.

Canada has also undertaken to continue providing relief from customs duties on some machinery and equipment and repair and replacement parts for such machinery and equipment not available from Canadian suppliers. Between now and January 1, 1989, Canada will examine this list of machinery and equipment with a view to adding to it. This will ensure that Canadian manufacturers seeking to modernize to take advantage of other provisions of the Agreement will be able to purchase new machinery and equipment at competitive prices.

Canadian and United States tariffs applied to products from other countries will be unchanged as a result of this Agreement. Both governments are participating in the Uruguay Round of Multilateral Trade Negotiations which could result in reductions or elimination of many of these tariffs. These reductions would, of course, form part of a larger package which would involve improved market access to the European Community, Japan and other developed, as well as developing, countries. These reductions will be addressed on their own merits and wholly separately from the bilateral Agreement.

The combined effect of eliminating both Canadian and U.S. tariffs will be to allow Canada's manufacturing industry to rationalize and modernize and become more competitive. Canadian companies will be able to increase their penetration of the U.S. market and of world markets in general. The result should be more and better jobs for Canadians.

Customs Matters

Whatever the level of tariffs, the way in which they are applied including provisions for granting duty remissions to importers, can affect trade flows. To ensure that the objectives of tariff elimination are achieved, Canada and the United States have also agreed to eliminate or regulate tariff-related programs which influence the flow of trade. The gradual elimination of most of these programs will ensure that by the end of the transition period, when all tariffs will have been eliminated, Canadian and U.S. companies will operate according to similar customs rules on bilateral trade. Both governments, however, will retain separate customs and tariff regimes for trade with third countries.

Specifically, the Agreement addresses customs user fees, duty drawbacks, and duty remissions.

The United States applies a customs user fee calculated as a percentage of the value of each import transaction (currently 0.17 percent). Even if the tariff is zero, the exporter must pay this amount when goods cross from Canada into the United States. This fee constitutes an additional tariff and increases the cost of exporting.

Article 403 provides that the customs user fee applied by the United States will be phased out on imports from Canada by January 1,

1994 and prevents either country from establishing a new customs user fee on imports of goods which meet the origin rules. Canadian exporters will save tens of millions of dollars with the elimination of this fee.

Both countries refund the customs duty levied on imported materials and components when these are incorporated into exported goods. This is called duty drawback. In the U.S., for example, foreign trade zones are often used as a means for U.S. exporters to avoid having to pay U.S. duties on imported components. Some of the advantages of the free-trade area, however, would be eroded if a U.S. producer could source some components from a third country, manufacture a final product in a U.S. foreign trade zone without paying any duty on these components and compete in Canada with a manufacturer who has paid Canadian duties on the same components. Accordingly, the Agreement provides for duty drawbacks on third-country materials and similar programs to be eliminated for bilateral trade after January 1, 1994.

There are two exceptions to the general drawback obligation. Drawbacks will continue to be permitted on citrus products. As well, duties paid on fabric imported and made up into apparel and subsequently exported to the other country can be recovered if the apparel does not qualify for duty-free treatment. Chapter Three establishes quotas for duty-free treatment for apparel made up from imported fabrics. Should trade rise above these levels, Canadian manufacturers using imported fabric will be able to apply for drawback of Canadian duties paid on fabric incorporated into apparel exported to the United States.

Canadian customs law permits duties on imports to be refunded to specific companies if these companies meet commitments (performance requirements) related to production, exports or employment. This practice is called duty waivers or remissions. The Agreement provides for the elimination of duty waivers wherever such waivers are tied to specific performance requirements such as production in one country or exports to the other except for automotive waivers as listed in Chapter Ten. No new customs duty waivers incorporating performance requirements can be introduced as of June, 1988, or whenever the U.S. Congress approves the Agreement, and all such customs duty waivers will be eliminated by January 1, 1998.

Customs Administration

Given the size of our existing bilateral trade, there is already extensive cooperation between Canadian and U.S. customs authorities. Article 406 and its annex provides for further cooperation by specifying a number of matters where it is not only desirable but necessary for the two customs authorities to work closely together. These matters include declarations of origin on imported goods, certificates of origin on exported goods, administration and enforcement, the uniform application of rules of origin, the facilitation of trade in the areas of statistics collection and documentation, as well as the operations of customs offices.

Import and Export Restrictions

Import or export quotas can be severely damaging to international trade by limiting the quantity which may be traded. In Article 407, Canada and the United States affirm their GATT obligations not to prohibit or restrict imports or exports of goods in bilateral trade except under strictly defined circumstances. Nothing in the Agreement, for example, in any way prevents Canada from prohibiting the import of pornographic materials (see chapter Twelve). Outside of such special circumstances, these obligations provide a guarantee that the benefits of tariff elimination will not be eroded by quotas or other restrictions. Unless specifically allowed by the Agreement, e.g., "grandfathered" or permitted under the GATT, existing quantitative restrictions will be eliminated, either immediately or according to a timetable.

Among those restrictions eliminated are the Canadian embargoes on used aircraft and used automobiles (provided in chapter Ten) and the U.S. embargo on lottery materials. Canada and the United States will retain their right to control log exports while the United States will retain marine transportation restrictions under the *Jones Act* (provided for in chapter Twelve). For shipbuilders, Canada has reserved the right to apply quantitative restrictions on U.S. vessels until such time as the United States removes the prohibitions under the *Jones Act* on Canadian vessels. Provincial laws governing the export of unprocessed fish caught off the East Coast have been safeguarded (also provided for in chapter Twelve). Both countries will continue to be able to apply import restrictions to agricultural goods where these are necessary to ensure the operation of a domestic supply management or support program.

Where either Canada or the United States applies restrictions on trade with other countries, it may limit or prohibit the pass-through of imports from those other countries into its own territory. It may also require that its exports to the other be consumed within the other's territory. Controls on exports to third countries for strategic reasons will thus continue to be enforced.

Export Taxes

Neither country applies export taxes as a matter of general policy. These render exporters less competitive and are highly disruptive of production and investment. Article 408 confirms existing practice by specifically prohibiting export taxes or duties on bilateral trade unless the same tax is applied on the same goods consumed domestically.

The 1986 Softwood Lumber Understanding, which requires Canada to collect an export tax on Canadian softwood exports to the United States until such time as the provincial governments have adjusted certain stumpage practices, is specifically grandfathered by Article 1910.

Other Export Measures

GATT obligations recognize that circumstances may arise where export restrictions are necessary. These circumstances include situations of short supply, conservation of natural resources where domestic production or consumption is also restrained and restrictions imposed in conjunction with domestic price stabilization schemes.

Article 409 requires that export restrictions for such purposes do not reduce the proportion of the good exported to the other Party relative to the total supply of the good compared to the proportion exported prior to the imposition of the restriction. Any such restriction must not be designed to disrupt normal channels of supply or proportions among specific goods being restricted. It prohibits the use of licenses, fees or other measures to charge higher prices for exports than for domestic sales (see also chapter Nine on energy).

Chapter Five: National Treatment

This chapter incorporates the fundamental national treatment obligation of the GATT into the Free-Trade Agreement. This means that once goods have been imported into either country, they will not be the object of discrimination. Such an obligation is an essential part of any Agreement eliminating trade barriers since it prevents their replacement by internal measures favouring domestic goods over imports. If such a provision were not part of the Agreement, exporters in either country would have no guarantee of equal treatment.

The practical effect of this chapter is to require that internal taxes, such as sales or excise taxes, cannot be higher on imported goods than on domestic goods and health and safety standards cannot be more rigorous for imported goods than for domestic goods. In other words, the obligation prevents either country from imposing internal taxes such as excise or sales taxes, regulations respecting matters such as, health and safety standards, laws respecting sale, purchase and use in a manner to discriminate against imported products. It is thus a guarantee that goods will be free of discrimination and will allow producers, traders, investors, farmers and fishermen to plan and invest with confidence.

National treatment does not mean that imported goods have to be treated in the same way in the foreign market as they are in their country of origin. For example, Canada can prohibit or restrict the sale of imported firearms so long as the sale of domestically produced firearms is also prohibited or restricted. Moreover, all goods, imported or domestic, must continue to meet Canadian requirements for bilingual labelling and metric measurement.

This chapter makes more explicit the GATT national treatment obligation to measures adopted by provinces or states. This means that a province or state cannot discriminate in respect of measures falling within its jurisdiction against imported products.

Chapter Six: Technical Barriers

The right to maintain regulations to protect human, animal and plant life, the environment or for a variety of other purposes is a sovereign issue for each country to decide. Such regulations for health, safety, environmental, national security and consumer protection reasons can, however, constitute severe barriers to trade, and unless there are rules to prevent their explicit use to impede trade, technical regulations can be highly protectionist trade measures.

In the Tokyo Round of Multilateral Trade Negotiations, an *Agreement on Technical Barriers to Trade* was reached which provides that technical regulations and standards including packaging and labelling requirements and methods for certifying conformity should not create unnecessary barriers to trade. No country is prevented from taking measures to ensure protection of human, animal or plant life or other measures so long as they are not applied to cause arbitrary or unjustifiable discrimination between imported or domestic goods.

In this chapter, Canada and the United States affirm their obligations under the GATT Agreement respecting federal government measures affecting industrial products (agricultural and fish standards are covered in chapter Seven).

This means that the two federal governments have agreed to avoid the use of standards-related measures as unnecessary obstacles to trade. Standards-related measures are defined to include specifications and regulations, standards and rules for certification systems that apply to goods, and processes and production methods. For example, the federal government can require that children's pyjamas be manufactured from fire-proof material, but it must impose this requirement on both imported and domestically produced pyjamas. Nothing in the Agreement prevents Canada from requiring bilingual labelling of goods, as long as both domestic and imported goods meet the same requirement.

The two governments will endeavour to make their respective standards-related measures more compatible to reduce the obstacles to trade and the costs of exporting which arise from having to meet different standards. A particular problem with plywood standards is addressed in chapter Twenty. Many standards-related measures are developed by private organizations in both Canada and the United States (such as the Canadian Standards Association or the Underwriters Laboratory) and the two governments will encourage these organizations to continue to work toward achieving greater compatibility in the standards they establish.

The methods by which products are tested for conformity with standards can, in themselves, constitute a barrier to trade. Hence, the two countries have agreed to recognize each others' laboratory accreditation systems and will not require that testing and inspection agencies and certification bodies be located, or make decisions within its territory in order to gain accreditation.

The formulation of standards is left to each Party. However, the chapter requires that, except in urgent cases, full texts of proposed federal standards-related measures be provided to the other country and that at least 60 days be allowed for those who would be affected to comment on any proposed federal measure before the measure takes effect.

Article 608 provides for further negotiations respecting the compatibility of standards-related measures, accreditation and the acceptance of test data.

Chapter Seven: Agriculture

Canadian farmers export almost $3 billion in agricultural products to the United States and sought conditions which would make their access to the U.S. market both more open and more secure. At the same time, they did not want to impair either existing marketing systems for dairy and poultry products or the right to implement new supply management programs and import controls in accordance with our international obligations.

The government thus had three objectives in the agricultural area: to improve access for farm products; to make that access more secure; and to preserve Canada's agricultural policy instruments. The Agreement meets all three objectives: there is an important package of trade liberalizing measures; agricultural products will benefit from the increased security of access flowing from the arrangements on dispute settlement; and nothing in the Agreement will in any way affect the right of the federal government and the provinces to introduce and maintain programs to protect and stabilize farm incomes.

The principal trade liberalizing elements agreed in agriculture are:

- Article 701: prohibition of export subsidies on bilateral trade. This marks the first time that any two governments have agreed to prohibitions on export subsidies in the agricultural sector and marks an important signal to others around the world;

- Article 701: elimination of Canadian Western Grain Transportation rail subsidies on exports to the United States shipped through Canadian west coast ports; the provision does not affect shipments through Thunder Bay or exports to third countries through west coast ports;

- Articles 401 and 702: the phased elimination of all tariffs over a period of ten years (Canada is allowed to restore temporarily tariffs on fresh fruits and vegetables for a 20-year period under depressed price conditions in order to give Canada's horticultural industry an opportunity to adjust to more open trading conditions). This snapback provision applies only if the average acreage under cultivation for that product is constant or declining. Acreage converted from wine-grape cultivation is not included in this calculation;

- Article 704: mutual exemption from restrictions under meat import laws, thus ensuring free trade in beef and veal. Canadian beef and veal producers have in the past found their exports limited as the U.S. triggered its meat import restrictions or sought voluntary export restraints. Both countries have agreed to consult and take measures to avoid diversion should either country apply its meat import law against third countries;

- Article 705: elimination of Canadian import licenses for wheat, barley and oats and their products when U.S. grain support levels become equal to Canadian grain support levels. Both countries retain the right to impose or re-impose restrictions on grains and grain products if imports increase significantly as a result of substantial change in grain support programs. Annex 705.4 sets out the method for calculating support levels;

- Article 706: the Canadian global import quotas on chicken, turkey and eggs have been set at average levels of actual imports over the past five years;

- Article 707: an exemption for Canada from any future quantitative import restrictions on products containing ten percent or less sugar. The U.S. enjoys a waiver under the GATT to impose restrictions if imports are interfering with U.S. price support programs. Without this exemption, further products could be included;

- Article 708: regulatory barriers resulting from technical regulations, the kind which in the past have frustrated the export of Canadian pork products, have been reduced. Over the next few years, both countries will seek to harmonize such technical regulations. As part of this Agreement, the U.S. will maintain an "open border policy" for meat inspection which will now be limited to occasional spot checks to ensure compliance with inspection requirements. Additionally, the United States has agreed to recognize the term canola oil as a trade name for rapeseed; and

- Article 710: GATT rights and obligations (including Article XI) are retained for all agricultural trade not specifically dealt with in the Agreement. For example, Canadian dairy farmers will continue to benefit from supply management programs since these are not affected by the Agreement and are consistent with Canada's GATT obligations.

Finally, the two governments agreed that some of the most pressing problems in the agricultural area go beyond Canada and the United States and will need the co-operation of all countries. For example, the stiff competition for grain export markets leading to ruinous export subsidies cannot be resolved solely on a bilateral basis. The two governments have, therefore, agreed to consult more closely with each other; to take account of each other's export interests when using export subsidies on sales to third markets; and to work together in the GATT to further improve and enhance trade in agriculture (Articles 701 and 709).

Canada's farmers will make real gains. By the end of the next decade, those agricultural and food products such as meat and livestock, grains and oilseeds, and potatoes, which we produce in abundance and which form the heart of our farm exports, will be able to compete on an equal footing in the huge American market without the burden of tariffs and other barriers at the border. At the same time, marketing systems, farm income stabilization and price support programs remain unimpaired by the Agreement.

Chapter Eight: Wine and Distilled Spirits

Chapter Eight provides for the reduction of barriers to trade in wine and distilled spirits which arise from measures related to their internal sale and distribution. It constitutes a partial derogation from the national treatment provisions of chapter Five. The specific measures covered concern listing, pricing, distribution practices, blending requirements and the standards and labelling requirements affecting distinctive products. The objective of the chapter is to provide over time equal treatment for Canadian and U.S. wine and distilled products in each other's market. Canadians will, as a result, enjoy greater access to a wide variety of California wines at competitive prices. The brewing industry is not covered by this chapter (but see chapter Twelve).

The chapter specifies that measures concerning listing for sale of wine and distilled spirits are to be transparent, treat Canadian and U.S. products in the same way and be based on normal commercial considerations. Any distiller or wine producer applying for a listing is to be informed promptly of listing decisions, given the reasons for any refusal and the right to appeal such a decision. Estate wineries in British Columbia which existed on Oct. 4, 1987 and which produce less than 30,000 gallons annually may be automatically listed in that province.

On pricing, the chapter allows a provincial liquor board or any other public body distributing wine and distilled spirits to charge the additional cost of selling the imported product. Differential charges on wine which exceed this amount are to be reduced over a seven-year period from 1989 through 1995. The method for calculating this differential is specified. Differential charges on distilled spirits which exceed this amount are to be eliminated immediately when the Agreement comes into force. All other discriminatory pricing measures are to be eliminated immediately.

On distribution, measures can be maintained which allow wineries or distilleries to limit sales on their premises to wines and spirits produced on those premises. Similarly, Ontario and British Columbia are not prevented from allowing private wine outlets existing on Oct. 4, 1987 to favour their own wine. The Quebec provision relating to in-province bottling of wine for sale in grocery stores is grandfathered.

Canada has agreed to eliminate any measure requiring that distilled spirits imported in bulk from the United States be blended with Canadian spirits.

The chapter provides for mutual recognition of Canadian Whiskey and U.S. Bourbon Whiskey as distinct products. This means that the U.S. will not allow the sale of any product as Canadian Whiskey unless it has been manufactured in Canada in accordance with Canadian laws. Canada will not permit the sale of any product as Bourbon Whiskey unless it has been manufactured in the United States in accordance with U.S. laws.

Chapter Nine: Trade in Energy

Over the past decade, bilateral trade in energy has assumed increasing importance to Canadians. Canada exports more than $10 billion in energy products annually, including oil, gas, electricity and uranium. Billions more are exported in the form of downstream products such as various oil and gas derivatives. That trade provides a livelihood for thousands of Canadians. Some of these exports, however, are limited or threatened by U.S. restrictions and regulatory actions, including restrictions on exports of upgraded Canadian uranium, discriminatory price actions on natural gas, tariffs and threatened import fees on crude oil and products, and threatened restrictions on electricity.

This chapter, which reproduces some of the provisions of chapter Four as they relate to energy goods, will secure Canada's access to the United States market for energy goods. The two countries have recognized that they have a common interest in ensuring access to each other's market and enhancing their mutual security of supply. They have, therefore, built on their existing GATT rights and obligations and agreed that, as each other's best customers, they should get fair treatment should there be any controls on energy commodities. Both remain free to determine whether and when to allow exports and may continue to monitor and license exports.

Article 902 affirms Canadian and U.S. rights and obligations under the GATT on trade restrictions in energy products. This includes a prohibition on minimum export or import price commitments. More particularly, the United States has agreed to eliminate all U.S. restrictions on the enrichment of Canadian uranium and Canada will eliminate the requirement for uranium to be processed before it is exported to the U.S. The United States has also agreed to end its total embargo on exports of Alaskan crude oil and allow Canadians to import up to 50,000 barrels a day. These commitments are described in Annex 902.5.

Where either Canada or the U.S. applies import or export restrictions to energy trade with other countries, it may limit or prohibit the pass-through of imports from those other countries into its own territory. It may also require, in such instances, that its exports to the other be consumed within the other's territory.

Article 903 on export taxes restates the obligation of chapter Four not to impose taxes or charges on exports unless the same tax is applied to energy consumed domestically. Article 904 on other export measures restates the obligations of chapter Four that export restrictions may not reduce the proportion of the good exported to the other Party relative to the total supply of the good, compared to the proportion exported prior to the imposition of the restriction. It also prevents the use of licences, fees or other measures to charge higher prices for exports when such restrictions are used for short supply, conservation or domestic price stabilization reasons.

This Article also provides that export restrictions not be designed to disrupt normal channels of supply or alter the product mix as between various types of specific energy goods exported to the other country. For example, if Canada in future decides to implement measures to limit the consumption of oil, it can reduce exports to the United States proportional to the total supply of oil available in Canada. Any such restrictions must not be designed to disrupt normal trade patterns.

The two countries have also agreed to allow existing or future incentives for oil and gas exploration and development in order to maintain the reserve base for these energy resources.

The chapter recognizes the important role played by the National Energy Board in Canada and the Federal Energy Regulatory Commission and the Economic Regulatory Administration in the United States. If discrimination inconsistent with this Agreement results from a regulatory decision, direct consultations can be held with a view to ending any discriminatory action, such as the decisions earlier this year by the Federal Regulatory Commission prohibiting Canadian suppliers of natural gas from passing all their shipment costs on to their customers.

In Annex 905.2, Canada undertakes to eliminate one of three price tests which the National Energy Board (NEB) applies to exports.

Through these tests, the NEB assesses whether all costs have been recovered, whether the offered price would not be less than the cost to Canadians for equivalent service, and whether the offered price would be materially less than the least cost alternative for the buying entity. It is this "least cost alternative test" only which is being eliminated.

The United States will require the Bonneville Power Administration to treat British Columbia Hydro no less favourably with respect to access to power transmission lines than utilities located outside the U.S. Pacific Northwest. The two governments state their expectation that Bonneville Power and British Columbia Hydro will continue to negotiate mutually beneficial arrangements on the use of power transmission lines.

Article 907 provides a tighter national security exception than is contained in the GATT and for the Agreement as a whole, while Article 908 indicates that the provisions of the *Agreement on an International Energy Program,* which governs trade in oil during tight supply conditions, take precedence over the provisions of this chapter.

Chapter Ten: Trade in Automotive Products

The automotive industry is the linchpin of Canadian manufacturing and the trade flow between Canada and the United States in autos is enormous. Autoworkers on both sides of the border have been beneficiaries of what has been our most important bilateral free-trade deal to date -- the Auto Pact. Throughout the negotiations, the Canadian government indicated that it was satisfied with the Auto Pact but was not averse to considering changes that would increase production, investment and employment in Canada. The Agreement meets these objectives.

The free and secure access to the U.S. market provided by the Auto Pact remains intact. The Auto Pact safeguards and the Canadian value-added commitments remain in place for the Big Three auto manufacturers.

Section XVII of Annex 301.2 provides that all vehicles traded under the Free-Trade Agreement will be subject to its rules of origin. Under the Auto Pact, qualified producers, as long as they meet the safeguards, can import vehicles and parts duty-free into Canada from anywhere in the world. Fifty percent of the direct production costs of any vehicle traded under the Free-Trade Agreement, however, will have to be incurred in Canada and the United States to qualify for duty-free treatment. Under the current rule governing exports to the U.S. under the Auto Pact, overhead and other indirect costs are included in the requirement that 50 percent of the invoice price be incurred in Canada or the U.S. The new rule is the equivalent of a 70 percent requirement on the old basis. To meet this test, assemblers will have to source more parts in North America, giving Canadian parts manufacturers increased opportunities.

The United States will accord vehicles and original equipment parts exported from Canada duty-free access if they meet the new rule of origin. Such goods now enjoy duty-free access under the Auto Pact. For northbound trade, Canadian manufacturers with Auto Pact status can import duty free under the Auto Pact (by satisfying the safeguards). Goods imported by all others under the FTA must meet the FTA rule if they wish to benefit from the declining bilateral tariff.

Chapter Ten addresses issues which are unique to the auto sector. It provides that each country will endeavour to administer the Auto Pact in the best interests of production and employment in Canada and the United States. It specifies that Canada shall not add to those Canadian manufacturers operating under the Auto Pact and comparable arrangements as of the entry into force of the Agreement.

There are separate provisions respecting other automotive duty waivers or remissions. Existing remissions cannot be extended to additional recipients, nor expanded, nor extended where such remissions apply to goods imported from other countries and are tied to performance requirements on automotive or other goods. Duty remissions earned through parts exports to the United States are ruled out upon entry into force of the Agreement, will be terminated by 1998 where the remissions depend on parts exports to any other countries. The current recipients of these waivers are listed in an annex, as are manufacturers who qualify under the Auto Pact.

Waivers or remissions committed prior to the Agreement's entry into force and tied to the value added contained in production in Canada other than for manufacturers qualifying under the Auto Pact are to be terminated by 1996.

Article 1003 provides for the phased elimination of the used car embargo. By 1993, any used automobile will be eligible for import into Canada from the United States.

These provisions taken together mean that:

- The Big Three and other qualified auto makers will be able to continue to benefit from their privileges under the Auto Pact and comparable arrangements to bring in vehicles and parts duty-free from all over the world as long as they continue to meet the Auto Pact production safeguards. They currently save $300 million annually in duties on their imports from third countries.

- Manufacturers listed in Annex 1002.1 Part 1 who can qualify for Auto Pact status in the 1989 model year will enjoy similar benefits.

- The Canadian government will continue to honour its commitments to provide duty waivers to companies with new production facilities in Canada to encourage them to source parts in Canada. This program and the rule of origin provisions in chapter Three will provide a strong incentive for offshore producers to purchase parts in Canada.

The two governments also agreed that some of the challenges facing the North American auto industry were more than a matter of negotiating a Free-Trade Agreement. They have, therefore, agreed to establish a select panel to advise the two governments on automotive issues (Article 1004).

Chapter Eleven: Emergency Action

A traditional feature of most trade Agreements is the ability of the Parties temporarily to impose restrictions (such as quotas or surcharges) otherwise inconsistent with the Agreement to deal with surges in imports causing serious injury to domestic producers. The ability to impose such emergency restrictions is often the key to gaining acceptance for the liberalizing provisions of an Agreement. The challenge is to circumscribe the right to take emergency action in such a manner as to prevent abuse. In a free-trade Agreement, once investors have taken steps to take advantage of the new opportunities, their expectations should not be frustrated by others who have not adjusted.

In chapter Eleven, the two governments have agreed to stringent standards for the application of emergency safeguards to bilateral trade. For the transition period only (i.e., until the end of 1998), either country may respond to serious injury to domestic producers resulting from the reduction of tariff barriers under the Agreement with a suspension of the duty reductions for a limited period of time or a return to the most-favoured-nation tariff level (i.e., the current tariff which may in future be reduced through multilateral negotiations). No measure can last more than three years or extend beyond December 31, 1998, except with the consent of both Parties. Any such action will also be subject to compen-sation by the other country, for example, through accelerated duty elimination on another product.

Additionally, Canada and the United States have agreed to exempt each other from global actions under GATT Article XIX except where the other's producers are important contributors to the injury caused by a surge of imports from all countries. This will mean that Canadian companies will no longer need to fear being sideswiped by an emergency action aimed largely at other suppliers, such as has happened in the case of specialty steel. Should either government take global emergency action, however, companies in the other country will not be allowed to rush in and take advantage of the situation. Any surge in exports in those circumstances may lead to their inclusion in the global action. Should the other Party be included in a global action either initially or subsequently, its exports will be protected against reductions below the trend line of previous bilateral trade with allowance for growth. Again, any emergency measures applied between the two countries will be subject to compensation.

For greater certainty and in order to help guide any deter-mination by domestic tribunals as to whether or not the other country is contributing importantly to any injury justifying a global measure, Article 1102 contains specific thresholds. Imports below five percent of total imports will not generally be considered to be substantial and will be excluded from any action. Imports above ten percent would be considered substantial and would be examined further to see whether they were an important cause of the serious injury from imports.

Any dispute as to whether the conditions for imposing a bilateral measure, for including the other Party in a global action or for the adequacy of compensation will be subject to binding arbitration after the action has been taken.

The provisions of this Chapter are important in establishing a more predictable climate for investors in both countries to take advantage of the Agreement, secure in the knowledge that their access to the other market will not be impaired by capricious action stemming from domestic complaints. They will be able to benefit from clear rules backed up by binding arbitration.

Chapter Twelve: Exceptions for Trade in Goods

As with the Chapter on emergency action, most trade agreements contain general exceptions. Such exceptions recognize that governments must retain some freedom of action to protect their legitimate national interests. In effect, they constitute a buffer zone without which binding international agreements could not be concluded between sovereign nations. For the part of the Agreement dealing with trade in goods, the two governments have agreed to incorporate the provisions of GATT Article XX and the grandfather provisions of the GATT's Protocol of Provisional Application. Most free-trade agreements have followed a similar practice.

GATT Article XX can justify import and export control measures, otherwise prohibited by the Agreement, for the following reasons:

- necessary to protect public morals (such as prohibitions on trade in pornographic material);

- necessary to protect human, animal or plant life or health (such as measures to protect the environment or endangered species);

- relating to trade in gold or silver;

- necessary to ensure compliance with domestic laws and regulations not otherwise inconsistent with the GATT (such as product standards);

- relating to the products of prison labour (producers should not have to compete with goods produced with prison labour);

- necessary to protect national treasures of artistic, historic or archaeological value; and

- undertaken in pursuance of an international commodity agreement (such as an international wheat or tin agreement).

Article XX also includes provisions relating to the preservation of commodities in short supply. These have been modernized and addressed in chapter Four (Border Measures) in the context of obligations relating to export measures and in chapter Nine for energy goods.

Finally, the provisions of Article XX are not absolute. They are subject to the requirement that they not be applied so as to constitute an arbitrary, unjustifiable or disguised restriction on trade. By virtue of their incorporation in the bilateral Agreement, any future dispute about the application of any measure on bilateral trade justified under this Article would be subject to the much better dispute resolution mechanism of this Agreement.

GATT's Protocol of Provisional Application was the instrument used by the original twenty-three signatories to bring the GATT into force. The signatories agreed that they would fully accept certain obligations insofar as they were not inconsistent with existing legislation on January 1, 1948. The most important policy swept up in the Protocol is the grandfathering of the United States *Jones Act* providing protection for the United States marine industry.

Chapter Twelve also includes a number of miscellaneous exceptions to the trade in goods chapters. The two governments have agreed to grandfather existing controls on the export of logs. In addition, East Coast provinces will be able to maintain existing provincial controls on the export of unprocessed fish. Both provisions will allow Canada to maintain policies aimed at upgrading these resources before export. With respect to restraints on the export of unprocessed fish caught off British Colombia, the two governments are pursuing, outside the Agreement, their rights and obligations under the GATT in light of the recent panel finding. Finally, Article 1204 grandfathers, subject to each Party's GATT rights, existing practices respecting the internal sale and distribution of beer.

Part Three
Government Procurement

The provisions on government procurement are contained in a separate part because a number of the general obligations respecting trade in goods do not apply, such as the national treatment obligations of chapter Five or the rules of origin of chapter Three. The coverage however is limited to goods, or services incidental to the delivery of goods.

Chapter Thirteen: Government Procurement

Chapter Thirteen marks important new progress in expanding the market opportunities for suppliers of goods to government markets. Canadians have proven themselves competitive suppliers of many commercial and industrial products to the United States. These include vehicles, scientific apparatus, aircraft equipment, mineral products, industrial machinery, plastic, rubber and leather products, electrical machinery, chemical products, power generation machinery, and heating and lighting equipment. The potential for increased sales by Canadian suppliers should thus be distributed widely across all regions of Canada.

The chapter broadens and deepens the obligations both countries have undertaken in the GATT Code, commits each country to work toward the multilateral liberalization of government procurement and to negotiate further improvements in the bilateral Agreement once multilateral negotiations are concluded.

The chapter increases the amount of procurement open for competition between Canadian and U.S. suppliers in each other's market. It lowers the threshold from U.S.$171,000 (about CDN $238,000), in the GATT Code, for purchases by Code-covered entities of covered goods to U.S.$25,000 (about CDN$33,000). All government purchases above this new threshold will be open to competition unless they are reserved for small business or excluded for reasons of national security.

In addition, the chapter makes substantial improvements upon the GATT Code in transparency procedures. It establishes jointly agreed principles, contained in Annex 1305.3, governing bid challenge procedures to ensure equitable and effective treatment for potential suppliers. An impartial reviewing authority will investigate situations where suppliers believe they have been unfairly treated and will ensure a timely decision. The reviewing authority will also be able to recommend changes in procurement procedures in accordance with the Agreement.

There are detailed provisions for the regular exchange of government procurement information. This will enable careful monitoring of the implementation of the chapter on an annual basis and will assist in resolving problems and providing the foundation for further negotiations in the GATT and bilaterally.

Annex 1304.3 reproduces the GATT Annex setting out for each country the purchasing entities whose purchases above the threshold are covered by both the GATT and this Agreement.

For the United States, 11 out of 13 government departments are covered by the GATT Code, with the only exceptions being the Departments of Energy and Transport. A total of 40 governmental agencies and commissions, as well as NASA and the General Services Administration (the common government purchasing agency) are included. Department of Defense purchases are covered within certain defined product categories such as vehicles, engines, industrial equipment and components, computer software and equipment, and commercial supplies.

For Canada, 22 government departments and 10 agencies are covered. Department of National Defence purchases of certain defined products, mainly non-military, are also covered. The Departments of Transport, Communications, and Fisheries and Oceans are not included.

Canada's access to U.S. defence procurement of military goods under the Defence Production Sharing Arrangements is not affected by this chapter.

Part Four
Services, Investment and Temporary Entry

Part Four contains the three ground-breaking chapters: services, business travel and investment.

Chapter Fourteen: Services

Trade in services represents the frontier of international commercial policy in the 1980s. Dynamic economies are increasingly dependent on the wealth generated by service transactions. International trade in services, of course, does not take place in a vacuum without rules and regulations. What it has lacked is a general framework of rules incorporating principles of general application such as those embodied in the GATT for trade in goods. Chapter Fourteen provides, for the first time, a set of disciplines covering a large number of service sectors.

The issue is also more than a matter of opening up service markets. It is no longer possible to talk about free trade in goods without talking about free trade in services because trade in services is increasingly mingled with the production, sale, distribution and service of goods. Companies today rely on advanced communications systems to co-ordinate planning, production, and distribution of products. Computer software helps to design new products. Some firms engage in-house, accountants, and engineers, some have 'captive' subsidiaries to handle their insurance and finance needs. In other words, services are both inputs for the production of manufactured goods (from engineering design to data processing) and necessary complements in organizing trade (from financing and insuring the transaction to providing installation and after-sales maintenance, especially critical for large capital goods).

The basic economic efficiency and competitiveness gains expected from the removal of barriers to trade in goods between Canada and the United States also apply to the service sectors. To achieve the same economic gains in services it was necessary to focus the negotiations on the nature of regulations that constitute trade barriers. In some cases the focus was the right of establishment where such a right is an economic pre-condition to supplying the service, for example, travel agencies. In other cases, the opportunities to foreigners to meet the ofessional licensing standards imposed by countries as a condition to ering the service, for example, architecture, was the focus.

In Article 1402, the two governments agree to extend the nciple of national treatment to the providers of a list of commercial vices established in Annex 1408. With the exception of transporion, basic telecommunications (such as telephone service) doctors, ntists, lawyers, childcare and government provided services (health, ucation and social services) most commercial services are covered. is means that Canada and the United States have agreed not to scriminate between Canadian and American providers of these rvices. Each will be treated the same. But this is not an obligation to rmonize. If Canada chooses to treat providers of one service fferently than does the United States, it is free to do so, as long as it es not discriminate between Americans and Canadians. Each vernment also remains free to choose whether or not to regulate and w to regulate.

The obligation to extend national treatment also does not mean e treatment has to be the same in all respects. For example, a Party ay accord different treatment for legitimate purposes such as nsumer protection or safety, so long as the treatment is equivalent in fect. Additionally, regulations cannot be used as a disguised striction on trade. Article 1403, for example, specifies that either vernment remains free to license and certify providers of specific rvices, but must ensure that such licensing requirements do not act as discriminatory barrier for persons of the other Party to meet.

The obligations are prospective, i.e., they do not require either vernment to change any existing laws and practices. Rather, the arties agree that in changing existing regulations for covered rvices, they will be guided by the obligation not to make such gulations any more discriminatory than they are already. However, y new regulations for covered services will have to conform fully to e national treatment obligation.

While there are no rules of origin for the services chapter, as ere are for trade in goods, the obligations are meant to extend enefits to Canadians and Americans. Article 1406, therefore, rovides that either Party remains free to deny the benefits of this aapter if it can demonstrate that a service is in fact being provided by provider who is a national of a third country. At the same time,

neither government is obliged to discriminate against providers
services from a third country.

Sectoral annexes clarify these general obligations for th
service sectors: architecture, tourism and enhanced telecommu
cations and computer services. Article 1405 provides scope for
two governments to negotiate more sectoral annexes in the future.

Transportation services (marine, air, trucking, rail and
modes) are not covered by the Agreement. In effect, existing arran;
ments, such as ICAO and the various air bilateral agreements, w
continue to govern bilateral relationships.

The new, general rules adopted for trade in services are a tr
blazing effort and could lay the foundation for further wc
multilaterally. Applying these rules prospectively will ensure that n
discrimination will not be introduced. This constitutes a major st
toward ensuring that open and competitive trade in services contim
between the two countries.

Chapter Fifteen: Temporary Entry for Business Persons

In this chapter, the two Parties establish a unique set
obligations to deal with an increasingly vexing problem
international trade. Export sales today require more than a go
product at a good price. They also require a good sales network ar
most of all, reliable after-sales service. Free and open tra
conditions, therefore, require not only that goods, services a
investments be treated without discrimination, but that the peo}
required to make sales and manage investments or provide before a
after service of those sales and investments should be able to mo
freely across the border. Furthermore, trade in professional a
commercial services cannot take place unless people can move free
across the border. The challenge, therefore, was to ensure th
immigration regulations would complement the rules governing t
movement of goods, services and investments, but would n
compromise the ability of either government to determine who m;
gain entry.

The government's objectives in this area were informed by t
increasing frustration experienced by Canadian entrepreneurs
making and servicing sales to their U.S. customers. Many we
experiencing delays and even outright denial of entry for what mo

nsidered normal business travel. Some resorted to setting up U.S.
bsidiaries, dealing through third parties, or conducting their
siness electronically. The result was lost sales, higher costs, lower
ficiency and foreclosed opportunities. In the absence of eased
strictions on border crossings, such frustrations were likely to
crease as barriers to trade in goods and services and investment are
duced and eliminated as a result of other chapters of the Agreement.

To solve this problem, the two governments adapted immi-
ation regulations to facilitate business travel. In chapter Fifteen, the
o governments take the necessary steps to ensure that business
rsons and enterprises will have the necessary access to each other's
arket in order to sell their goods and services and supply after sales
rvice to their customers.

The agreed rules are based on reciprocal access for Canadian
d American business travellers to the other market. National laws
d regulations governing their entry will be liberalized and entry
ocedures will be quick and simple. In order to limit the application
f this general rule to genuine business travellers, the two
overnments have divided business travel into four categories and
vered seven specific types of activities. These are set out in detail in
e annexes to the chapter.

In order to gain temporary entry under the terms of the
greement to the United States, therefore, Canadian business
avellers must qualify for entry generally (i.e., meet normal health
nd safety requirements) and indicate the nature of their business (i.e.,
hether entering as a Business Visitor, as a Professional, as a Trader
r Investor, or as an Intra-Company Transferee);

In addition, a Professional must be on the list of professions set
ut in Schedule 2 of the Annex . A Business Visitor must also state the
pecific purpose of the visit and seven general types of activities are set
ut in Schedule 1 of the Annex:

- ° Research and Design
- ° Growth, Manufacture and Production
- ° Marketing
- ° Sales
- ° Distribution
- ° After Sales Service
- ° General Services

For other categories of business travellers, current restrictions, su⟨
as the need to gain prior approval or to meet a labour certification te⟨
would no longer apply to Canadians.

As they gain experience with the Agreement as a whole and wi⟨
the specific provisions of this chapter, the two governments w⟨
consider ways to improve the coverage and operation of these ne⟨
procedures. The dispute settlement provisions of the Agreement c⟨
be invoked if there is a clear pattern of discrimination in t⟨
administration of the entry procedures.

Chapter Sixteen: Investment

A hospitable and secure investment climate is indispensable ⟨
the two countries are to achieve the full benefits of reducing barrie⟨
to trade in goods and services. Chapter Sixteen establishes a mutual⟨
beneficial framework of principles sensitive to the national interests ⟨
both countries with the objective that investment flow more free⟨
between Canada and the United States and that investors be treated in ⟨
fair and predictable manner.

The basic obligation is to ensure that future regulation ⟨
Canadian investors in the United States and of American investors ⟨
Canada results in treatment no different than that extended to domest⟨
investors within each country. This basic principle is qualified on t⟨
basis of existing practice and is translated into the following specifi⟨
undertakings:

- Article 1602: national treatment on the establishment of ne⟨
  businesses. Canadian investors in the United States and U.⟨
  investors in Canada will be subject to the same rules as domesti⟨
  investors when it comes to establishing a new business.

- Article 1602 and Article 1607: more liberal rules on th⟨
  acquisition of existing businesses. Canada retains the right t⟨
  review the acquisition of firms in Canada by U.S. investors, b⟨
  has agreed to phase in higher threshold levels for direc⟨
  acquisitions. Article 1607 provides that the review threshol⟨
  for direct acquisitions will be raised in four steps to $15⟨
  million by 1992. At that time, about three-quarters of total non⟨
  financial assets in Canada now reviewable will still b⟨
  reviewable. For indirect acquisitions, which involve th⟨
  transfer of control of one foreign-controlled firm to another

the review process will be phased out over the same period. These changes to the Investment Canada review process will not apply to the oil and gas and uranium sectors.

- Article 1602: national treatment once established, i.e., the conduct, operation and sale of U.S.-owned firms in Canada or Canadian-owned firms in the United States will be subject to the same rules as firms owned by domestic investors. Both governments are completely free to regulate the ongoing operation of business enterprises in their respective juris-dictions under, for example, competition law, provided that they do not discriminate.

- Article 1603: limits on certain performance requirements. Both countries have agreed to prohibit investment-related performance requirements (such as local content and import substitution requirements) which significantly distort bilateral trade flows. The negotiation of product mandate, research and development, and technology transfer requirements with investors, however, will not be precluded. Moreover, this Article does not preclude the negotiation of performance requirements attached to subsidies or government procurement.

- Article 1605: due process on expropriation. If either government chooses to nationalize an industry to achieve some public policy goal, it is obligated to acquire foreign-controlled firms on the basis of due process and based on the payment of fair and adequate compensation.

- Article 1606: no restrictions on the patriation of profits or the proceeds of a sale other than those necessary to implement domestic laws of general application, such as bankruptcy laws, the regulation of securities or balance-of-payment measures.

These undertakings are prospective (i.e., applied to future changes in laws and regulations only). Existing laws, policies and practices are grandfathered, except where specific changes are required (Article 1607). The practical effect of these obligations, therefore, is to exempt the oil and gas and uranium sectors from changes to the *Investment Canada Act* (Annex 1607.3) and to freeze the various exceptions to national treatment provided in Canadian and U.S. law (such as the restrictions on foreign ownership in the communications and transportation industries). Additionally, both

governments remain free to tax foreign-owned firms on a differen
basis than domestic firms provided this does not result in arbitrary c
unjustifiable discrimination (Article 1609) and to exempt the sale c
Crown-owned firms from any national treatment obligations (Articl
1602). Finally, the two governments retain some flexibility in th
application of the national treatment obligations (Article 1602). The
need not extend identical treatment as long as the treatment i
equivalent (Article 1602).

The definitions are critical to understanding the operation o
this chapter. While they are complicated, they make it clear t
investors exactly who benefits or is affected by the operationa
Articles.

To make the chapter work, the two governments have agreed t
allow monitoring of foreign investment and to resolve any dispute
under the dispute settlement provisions of the Agreement, with th
exception that any review decisions by Investment Canada will not b
subject to dispute settlement. They have also agreed to work togethe
in the Uruguay Round of Multilateral Trade Negotiations on trade
related investment rules.

The freer flow of investment across the border will allow for th
creation of new jobs and wealth in both Canada and the United States
The hospitable investment environment in Canada enhanced throug
the investment provisions, as well as by the operation of th
Agreement as a whole, will ensure that adjustment and economi
growth proceed in an efficient manner but one which is sensitive to th
needs of individuals, regions and sectors.

Part Five
Financial Services

Chapter Seventeen: Financial Services

Trade is very important to Canada's financial services industr
and, through its financial institutions, Canada is well represented i
international financial markets. Among the larger groups of majo
financial services firms, the Canadian banks probably generate th
largest share of foreign income and a considerable amount of tha
income is related to their U.S. operations and activities.

Canadian banks have been active in the U.S. for a long time
while U.S. banks have only been able to provide a full range of
banking services in Canada since 1980. Chapter Seventeen preserves
the access that our respective financial institutions have to each other's
market. Also, both Canada and the United States have agreed to
continue liberalizing the rules governing their respective financial
markets and to extend the benefits of such liberalization to institutions
controlled by the other Party.

Prior to 1978, Canadian and other foreign banks were generally
permitted to operate in more than one state. Indeed, Canadian banks
had, and still have, retail and other banking operations in a number of
states, unlike many of their U.S. competitors. These privileges,
however, were subject to review after ten years. These privileges have
been "grandfathered" indefinitely in Article 1702.

In the area of securities, Canadian banks in the United States will
be able to underwrite and deal in securities of Canadian governments
and their agents. Up until now, because of the 50-year old *Glass-
Steagall Act* which separates commercial banking from the securities
business, only dealers unaffiliated with a bank could underwrite these
securities in the United States. Accordingly, a new business opportunity for Canadian banks has been created. At the same time, an
important commitment from the United States will help bridge the gap
between the pace of regulatory change in financial markets that has
opened up between Canada and the United States. For the future,
Canadian financial institutions are guaranteed, by Article 1702, that
they will receive the same treatment as that accorded United States
financial institutions with respect to amendments to the *Glass-Steagall
Act*.

Article 1703 exempts U.S. firms and investors from some
aspects of the federal "10/25" rule such that they will be treated the
same as Canadians. The rule prevents any single non-resident from
acquiring more than 10 percent of the shares, and all non-residents
from acquiring more than 25 percent of the shares of a federally-
regulated Canadian-controlled financial institution. The 10 percent
limitation on any individual shareholder resident or non-resident will
continue to be applied to the larger banks and thereby control of our
financial system will be maintained in Canadian hands.

Additionally, U.S. bank subsidiaries in Canada will be exempted
from the current 16 percent ceiling on the size of the foreign bank

sector. Finally, all U.S. applications to establish operations in Canad
have been subject to review. No changes to this review process a
required. U.S. applications will continue to be reviewed on a case-by-
case basis to ensure the suitability of the applicant, that it can make
positive contribution to Canada's financial markets, and that prudenti
concerns are met.

Financial institutions, other than insurance, are not covered b
the dispute settlement procedures of the Agreement. Rather, bo
Parties have agreed to consult and these consultations will take plac
between the Canadian Department of Finance and the United State
Department of the Treasury.

The financial services chapter builds on the federal gover
ment's commitment to provide more competition among financi
institutions with the resultant benefits to consumers. At the same tim
control of our financial system will remain in Canadian hands while
new business opportunity has been opened up for our banks in the U.S

Part Six
Institutional Provisions

Part Six contains both the general dispute settlement provisio
and the special arrangements for dealing with antidumping an
countervailing duties. In addition, this Part creates the institution
framework for managing and implementing the trade Agreement.

Chapter Eighteen: Institutional Provisions

This chapter establishes the necessary institutional provisions
provide for the joint management of the Agreement and to avoid an
settle any disputes between the Parties respecting the interpretation
application of any element of the Agreement. Its essential features a
economy, joint decision-making and effective dispute resolution. I
basic objective is to promote fairness, predictability and security b
giving each Partner an equal voice in resolving problems throug
ready access to objective panels to resolve disputes and authoritativ
interpretations of the Agreement.

To ensure that the Agreement is effectively implemented an
enforced, chapter Eighteen provides for:

- mandatory notification of any measure (Article 1803);

- mandatory provision of information to the other party on any measure, whether or not it has been notified(Article 1803);

- consultations at the request of either party concerning any measure or any other matter which affects the operation of the Agreement, with a view to arriving at a mutually satisfactory resolution (Article 1804);

- referral to a Canada-United States Trade Commission, should resolution through consultations fail (Article 1805); and

- use of dispute settlement procedures should the Commission fail to arrive at a mutually satisfactory resolution. Procedures are:

   ○ compulsory arbitration, binding on both parties, for disputes arising from the interpretation and application of the safeguards provision (Article 1103);

   ○ binding arbitration in all other disputes (Article 1806) where both parties agree; and

   ○ panel recommendations to the Commission, which, in turn, is mandated to agree on a resolution of the dispute (Article 1807).

These provisions are in addition to the special dispute settlement mechanism established in Chapter Nineteen to deal with antidumping and countervailing duty issues.

The Commission is composed of equal representatives of both parties. The principal representative of each party is the ministerial rank official responsible for international trade matters, or his or her designee. Regular Commission meetings are held once a year, alternating between the two countries. As a practical matter, the day-to-day work of the Commission will be by officials of the two governments responsible for individual issues acting as working groups mandated by the Commission.

Arbitrators are selected by the Commission on such terms and in accordance with such procedures as it may adopt. Panels are composed of five members: two Canadians, two Americans, and a fifth member chosen jointly. Panelists are normally chosen from a roster developed by the Commission. Each Party chooses its national members, while the Commission chooses the fifth member. If the Commission is unable to agree on a choice, the other four members choose; should that fail the fifth member is selected by lot.

Panels are allowed to establish their own rules of procedure, unless the Commission decides otherwise. There will be a right for at least one hearing before the panel, and the opportunity to provide written submissions and rebuttal arguments. Panel proceedings are confidential. All consultations and panel proceedings are subject to time limits, to ensure prompt resolution of disputes.

In the case of arbitral awards, the aggrieved Party has the right to suspend the application of equivalent benefits under the Agreement to the non-complying Party. In cases where the Commission does not reach agreement after receiving a Panel recommendation, and the dispute involves a measure that the aggrieved Party believes impairs its fundamental rights or anticipated benefits under the Agreement, it can suspend the application of equivalent benefits until the issue is resolved.

The combined effect of the institutional provisions and the three forms of dispute settlement (binding settlement of disputes over trade remedy actions, mutually agreed binding arbitration, and recommendatory panel procedures), will make Canada an equal partner in the resolution of disputes and provide for fair and effective solutions to difficult problems. Canadians will know what the rules are and can be confident that they will have a voice in how they will be applied.

Chapter Nineteen: Binational Dispute Settlement in Antidumping and Countervailing Duty Cases

In negotiating a better and more balanced framework for the conduct of trade between Canada and the United States, Canada sought to increase predictability and security for Canadian exporters to the United States. Without this predictability, Canadian companies cannot be sufficiently confident to take advantage of other provisions of the Agreement, such as the elimination of tariffs or improved access to government procurement.

Trade remedy procedures, such as antidumping and countervailing duty petitions, can pose a serious threat to predictability and

:curity of access. In recent years, actions taken under U.S. trade
:medy laws against Canadian exports have had a detrimental impact
n investment and employment in Canada, and have become a major
ritant in Canada-U.S. relations.

In this chapter, the two governments agree that in order for both
des to take equal advantage of the benefits of the Agreement, there
ill be need for conditions of fair competition to ensure that economic
ctors on both sides of the border have equal access to the whole free-
ade area established by the Agreement. This will be achieved as a
:sult of a three-track set of obligations:

- the development over a five- to seven-year period of mutually
  advantageous rules governing government subsidies and private
  anti-competitive pricing practices such as dumping, which are
  now controlled through the unilateral application of countervailing and antidumping duties;

- bilateral review of any changes in existing countervailing or
  antidumping laws and regulations for consistency with the
  GATT and the object and purpose of the Agreement; and

- the replacement of judicial review by domestic courts of
  countervailing and antidumping final orders by a bilateral
  panel.

Article 1907 provides that the two governments will work
owards establishing a new regime to address problems of dumping
nd subsidization to come into effect no later than at the end of the
eventh year. During the course of the current negotiations, the two
ides recognized that developing a new regime was a complex task and
vould require more time. The goal of any new regime, however, will
e to obviate the need for border remedies, as are now sanctioned by
he GATT Antidumping and Subsidies Codes, for example, by
leveloping new rules on subsidy practices and relying on domestic
ompetition law. Thus the goal of the two governments remains the
stablishment of a new regime to replace current trade remedy law
vell before the end of the transition period.

In the meantime, chapter Nineteen includes provisions to
revent abuse of the current system, thus allowing Canadian exporters
o compete in the U.S. market on a more secure, predictable and
quitable footing. In Article 1904, the two governments have agreed

to a unique dispute settlement mechanism that guarantees the impartia
application of their respective antidumping and countervailing dut
laws. Either government may seek a review of an antidumping c
countervailing duty determination by a bilateral panel with bindin
powers. This will mean that producers in both countries will continu
to have the right to seek redress from dumped or subsidized import:
but any relief granted will be subject to challenge and review by
binational panel which will determine whether existing laws wei
applied correctly and fairly. Canadian producers who have in the pa.
complained that political pressures in the United States have dispose
U.S. officials to side with complainants will now be able to appeal to
bilateral tribunal.

Findings by a panel will be binding on both governments
Should the panel determine that the law was properly applied, th
matter is closed. If it finds that the administering authority (th
Department of Commerce or the International Trade Commission i
the United States or the Department of National Revenue or th
Canadian Import Tribunal in Canada) erred on the basis of the sam
standards as would be applied by a domestic court, it can send the issu
back to the administering authority to correct the error and make
new determination.

In order to provide symmetry in the application of pane
reviews, both governments will amend their law to allow all fina
decisions to be subject to bilateral review.

Panelists who will review antidumping and countervailing dut
decisions will be chosen from a roster of individuals who hav
previously agreed to act as panelists. Because of the judicial nature o
the review, the majority of panelists will be lawyers. Nevertheless, th
procedures allow for at least two non-lawyers who can bring othe
expertise to bear on any panel decision, such as business experience.

Panels must be acceptable to both sides. Each government wil
choose two panelists and jointly choose the fifth; if they cannot agree
the four chosen panelists will pick a fifth from the roster; if the
cannot agree, the fifth panelist will be chosen by lot. Each governmen
will be able to exercise two peremptory challenges of panelists chose
by the other side, for example, by indicating that a proposed panelist i
not suitable to act on a particular issue.

Decisions will be rendered quickly based on strict time limits built into the procedures. These limits are sufficiently generous to allow the Parties opportunity to develop arguments and to challenge the arguments of the other side. While only the two governments can seek the establishment of a panel, as a practical matter, many of the issues will involve private parties and these will be allowed to make representations before the panel. In addition, both governments are obligated to invoke the panel procedure if petitioned by private parties.

To ensure fairness and the integrity of the process, procedures have been developed to address any potential for the appearance of unfairness or corruption. In the unlikely event that a panelist has a conflict of interest or there has been a serious miscarriage of justice, either government can invoke an extraordinary challenge procedure involving a panel of three former judges who will determine whether or not the allegations are valid and whether or not a new panel will be required to review the issues.

The two governments will establish a small secretariat to administer these review procedures and to give aggrieved Parties ready access to information. Additionally, they will work out detailed rules of procedures for panels and a code of conduct for panelists.

The two governments agreed in Article 1903 that changes to existing antidumping and countervailing duty legislation apply to each other only following consultation and if specifically provided for in the new legislation. Moreover, either government may ask a bilateral panel to review such changes in light of the object and purpose of the Agreement, their rights and obligations under the GATT Antidumping and Subsidies Codes and previous panel decisions. Should a panel recommend modifications, the Parties will consult to agree on such modifications. Failure to reach agreement gives the other Party the right to take comparable legislative or equivalent executive action or terminate the Agreement.

The combined effect of bilateral review of existing law and the development of a new set of rules will be to ensure that by the time all tariffs are removed and other aspects of the Agreement phased in, Canadian firms will have not only more open access, but also more secure and more predictable access. At the same time, Canada's capacity to pursue regional development and social welfare programs remains unimpaired. Indeed, it has been strengthened.

Part Seven
Other Provisions

Chapter Twenty: Other Provisions

This chapter contains a range of miscellaneous provisions. Some deal with specific issues (such as intellectual property or cultural industries) or address an existing irritant in bilateral relations (such as cable retransmission rights) while others establish a general rule which affects the application of other chapters in the Agreement (such as balance-of-payment measures or the treatment of monopolies).

In Article 104 of chapter One, the Parties agreed on a general rule of interpretation that, where there is a conflict, the trade Agreement takes precedence over all other agreements unless provided otherwise in a particular chapter. In Article 2001, the Parties agree that the provisions of the 1980 tax convention between them takes precedence over the trade Agreement.

In Article 2002, the two governments affirm their rights and obligations under the GATT, the International Monetary Fund and the OECD Code of Liberalization of Capital Movements with respect to balance-of-payments measures. In effect, the two governments agree that should either find it necessary to apply exchange controls or take trade actions (such as a surcharge or quota) to counteract a serious deterioration in its balance-of-payments position, it will do so in manner consistent with these multilateral agreements. Additionally, they agree that they will not use balance-of-payments measures as a disguised restriction on trade, thus reiterating their multilateral commitments.

Article 2003 reproduces the standard national security clause of the GATT which applies to the rights and obligations provided in all but two chapters: energy, and government procurement. In the case of energy, the two governments have agreed on a more limited national security provision and the procurement chapter relies on the national security provision of the GATT Code on Government Procurement.

All international trade and economic agreements contain a national security provision giving the Parties sufficient flexibility to deal with national emergencies, to ensure that no provision of the Agreement can be interpreted to require a government to compromise classified material, to limit trade in military goods or not to meet its commitments under the United Nations Charter.

During the course of the negotiations, the two governments worked on an overall framework covering the protection of intellectual property rights (trademarks, copyright, patents, industrial design and trade secrets). In the end, a substantive chapter was dropped. Nevertheless, in Article 2004, the two governments agree to continue to cooperate and work toward better international intellectual property rules, particularly in the Uruguay Round of Multilateral Trade Negotiations where a working group on trade-related intellectual property issues has been established.

From the beginning of the negotiations, Canadians expressed concern that an agreement might erode the government's capacity to encourage and help Canada's cultural industries (film and video, music and sound recording, publishing, cable transmission and broadcasting) and thus to contribute to the development of Canada's unique cultural identity. In order to remove any ambiguity that Canada's unique cultural identity remains untouched by the Agreement, the two governments agreed in Article 2005 on a specific provision indicating that, with four very limited exceptions, nothing in this Agreement affects the ability of either Party to pursue cultural policies. The specific exceptions are:

- the elimination of tariffs on any inputs to, and products of, the cultural industries, such as musical instruments, cassettes, film, recording tape, records and cameras (Article 401);

- any requirement to sell a foreign-owned enterprise engaged in a cultural activity acquired indirectly through the purchase of its parent will be balanced by an offer to purchase the enterprise at fair open market value (paragraph 4 of Article 1607);

- both Parties will provide copyright protection to owners of programs broadcast by distant stations and re-transmitted by cable companies; this undertaking will be on a non-discriminatory basis; after Canadian legislation is implemented there will be an opportunity for further review of outstanding issues in both countries (Article 2006);

- the requirement that a magazine or newspaper must be typeset and printed in Canada in order for advertisers to be able to deduct their expenses for advertising space in that magazine will be eliminated (Article 2007).

In Article 2008 and an agreed exchange of letters, the two governments address a long-standing irritant involving plywood standards. The Canada Mortgage and Housing Corporation will decide by March 15, 1988 whether to allow the use of C-D grade plywood (a U.S. standard) for use in housing it finances. If it agrees, a series of tariff concessions will begin to be implemented on January 1, 1989. If not, the issue will be placed before a panel of experts. Once the panel has completed its work, the two governments will determine how to implement the tariff concessions specified in Article 2008.

In Article 2009, the two governments agree to grandfather the 1986 Memorandum of Understanding on Softwood Lumber. That Memorandum provided that Canada would apply a tax on the export of softwood lumber to the United States until such time as the producing provinces had adjusted certain stumpage practices.

Most trade agreements contain provisions to deal with policy measures which either government may adopt which, while technically not inconsistent with the obligations of the Agreement, have the effect of nullifying or impairing benefits that could have been reasonably expected under the Agreement. The most obvious such measure is the establishment of a monopoly or state enterprise. A government can, for example, instead of regulating an industry, establish a state enterprise and give it monopoly powers. If the sole purpose of the establishment of such an enterprise is to evade an obligation under the Agreement, the other Party can legitimately cry foul. Article 2010 establishes rules governing the establishment of monopolies (based on similar provisions in Article XVII of the GATT) while Article 2011 (based on Article XXIII of the GATT) provides a framework to address any claim of nullification and impairment.

Part Eight
Final Provisions

Chapter Twenty-One: Final Provisions

In Articles 2101 and 2102, the two governments agree to exchange the necessary statistical information and to publish all necessary information to facilitate implementation and administration of the Agreement. This chapter provides for annexes and amendments and the duration and entry into force of the Agreement. The Agreement will remain in effect indeterminately. Due to a provision in the U.S. fast-track approval procedures, any agreement brought forward under its provisions must contain a six-month termination clause.

Agreed Letters

The three letters set out understandings reached between the governments during the course of the negotiations on matters that require attention before the Agreement enters into force. The first letter reconfirms the understanding on a standstill between October 4, 1987 and the entry into force of the Agreement on actions not in keeping with the spirit of the Agreement. The second ensures that in case either government fails to implement the Harmonized System (the system by which goods are classified and upon which the tariff cuts are based) before the entry force of the Agreement, that the tariff reductions would still occur under the existing classification system. The third deals with the evaluation of American plywood standards for use in housing financed by Canada Mortgage and Housing Corporation. It links tariff reductions for plywood to the outcome of the CMHC assessment.

BIBLIOGRAPHIC ESSAY

One is always more in debt to the ideas of others than one realizes. This brief bibliographical essay is an attempt to acknowledge that at least partially.

The first three chapters of the book draw extensively on the flurry of articles, speeches and debates that constituted Canada's 1988–89 free trade trauma. Specific references are impossible for many of the interesting ideas that arose. However some do stand out. A 1963 study by Sperry Lea for the Canadian-American Committee, entitled "A Canada-U.S. Free Trade Arrangement: Survey of Possible Characteristics," contained a particularly helpful appendix on the history of Canada-U.S. trade negotiations. A paper entitled "An Historical Overview of Canada-U.S. Trade Relations," presented by Earl Fry at a Conference on Trade Liberalization in Montreal on October 30, 1986, also helped with the historical perspective. The multiple publications of Canada's Royal Commission on the Economic Union and Development Prospects for Canada, known as the Macdonald Commission, provided a particularly rich vein of analytical background. This commission was instrumental in propelling Canada into free trade discussions with the United States. Once the Free Trade Agreement had been initialled, Canada appointed an Advisory Council on Adjustment which reported on schedule and under budget on March 28, 1989. The Council's report, "Adjusting to Win," was an eloquent plea for positive training programs to help people pursue the opportunities created by globalization and free trade.

I found *The Economist*'s "Under Construction: A Survey of 1992," (July 8–14, 1989) issue particularly helpful in dealing with the Europe 1992 initiative. Thre were also some interesting ideas and data in the February 1989 publication, "Europe 1992: The Single Market Programme and Canadian Business," by the *Canadian Labour Market and Productivity Centre*. Again, there have been a lot of conference speeches during 1989 which have added a good deal of flavor to the Europe 1992 initiative.

F. A. Hayek's book, *The Fatal Conceit* (University of Chicago Press, 1988), gave me confidence to write about the ideological aspects of free trade. Hayek's support of the role of tradition in economic progress and his rejection of exclusive reliance on short-term incrementalism could have helped Canada to articulate its free trade debate more clearly. Supporters tended to lean on traditional beliefs in the efficacy of more open competition. They saw free trade as a leap of faith. Opponents tended to rely on more immediate arguments about the job impact on specific industries. They wanted guaranteed measurable results. After participating in Canada's free trade debate, I found Hayek's ideas uniquely relevant, particularly his views on the limits to rationality and empiricism. I wish I had read Hayek before the debate.

There has been so much written about globalization in the last five years that we can soon expect a partial backlash as in Michael Schrage's article in the July–August 1989 issue of the *Harvard Business Review* entitled "A Japanese Giant Rethinks Globalization." Among the most useful articles about globalization itself were Herbert Henzler and Wilhelm Rall's "Facing Up to the Globalization Challenge" (*The McKinsey Quarterly*, Fall 1986); Gunnar Hedlund's "The Hypermodern MNC—A Heterarchy?"

(*Human Resource Management,* Spring 1986); and Christopher A. Bartlett and Sumantra Ghoshal's "Organizing for Worldwide Effectiveness: The Transnational Solution" (*California Management Review,* Fall 1988). What these papers had in common was a regard for the limits of globalization and how to interpret them for particular industries, and a regard for the dangers to the corporation as a whole of emasculating overseas subsidiaries. Kenichi Ohmae's article "Planting for a Global Harvest" in the July-August 1989 issue of the *Harvard Business Review* reinforced the view that successful international companies have to adapt their plants and marketing practices to local capacities and markets around the world. It was probably Ohmae's 1985 Book, *Triad Power* (The Free Press, New York), that sparked the globalization debate in the first place. The simple recognition that Japan, the EEC and North America together account for over half the world's GNP started minds thinking. And Ohmae's suggestion that successful firms of the future must develop an insider presence in all three regions in order to circumvent protectionism and to stay abreast of technology, markets and competition got firms moving globally in a more committed way. Jeremy Main's article "How to Go Global—and Why" in the August 28, 1989, issue of *Fortune* was a straightforward endorsement of globalization, but in its global checklist it introduced the word "glocalize." Attributed to the Japanese, it tries to capture the idea of a combination of global strategic decision making and local tactical decision making.

Many of the publications about the impact of globalization on subsidiaries are Canadian, but certainly not all. Louis Kraar's article in the May 22, 1989, issue of *Fortune,* "North America's New Trade Punch," describes how several Canadian subsidiaries have positioned themselves to play an important role in their companies' strategies. Bartlett and Ghoshal's "Tap Your Subsidiaries for Global Reach" in the November-December 1986 issue of the *Harvard Business Review* categorized the possible roles of subsidiaries as strategic leaders, contributors, implementers or black holes according to the importance of the subsidiary's market and the competence of the subsidiary's management. Unfortunately, they placed Canadian subsidiaries in the role of implementers, but that was before the Free Trade Agreement changed the effective market open to Canadian subsidiaries. Their subsequent book "Managing across Borders—The Transnational Solution" (Harvard Business School Press, 1989), emphasizes the potential contribution of subsidiaries to the corporation as a whole, and devotes considerable attention to how to strengthen subsidiary roles without losing the advantages of global efficiency. My own article in the Fall 1987 issue of the *Sloan Management Review*, entitled "Managing Canadian Subsidiaries in a Free Trade Environment," discussed two forms of subsidiary specialization—rationalization and world product mandate. It argued for more of the latter and less of the former as long as subsidiaries had the managerial and technical depth to handle the challenge. In W. Chan Kim's article "Competition and the Management of Host Government Intervention" (*Sloan Management Review*, Spring 1987) the argument was made that the need for local adaptation increases as products age. The article recommended strong subsidiary boards of directors, more joint decision making bodies, and the use of parent-subsidiary executive seminars to promote better understanding and better organization-wide decision making.

Four articles were particularly helpful among Canadian publications. Alan Rugman and Alain Verbeke's "Strategic Responses to Free Trade" takes the position that most Canadian subsidiaries of American firms will maintain their competitive strengths under the Free Trade Agreement. Canadian fears of subsidiary plant shutdowns and massive transformation are, from this perspective, greatly exaggerated. James Fleck and Joseph D'Cruz, on the other hand, took the view in their article "Strategies for U.S. Subsidiaries after Free Trade," that U.S. multinationals would have to alter the missions of their Canadian subsidiaries to help them adjust to global developments. They went on to make a number of recommendations to Canadian subsidiary CEO's for managing the transition. Both of these articles are featured in *Business Strategies and Free Trade* (Policy Study No. 5, C. D. Howe Institute, May 1988), edited by Maureen Farrow and Alan M. Rugman.

Harold Crookell and Paul Bishop in their article "Specialization and Foreign Investment in Canada" in Volume 2 of the Macdonald Commission's *Canadian Industry in Transition* (University of Toronto Press, 1986), made the point that globalization trends were pressing Canadian subsidiaries to focus and specialize in order to become more competitive internationally. Thomas Poynter and Roderick White took the position in their article "Organizing for Worldwide Advantage" (*Business Quarterly*, Summer 1989) that subsidiaries have to strive for a reasonable balance between local and global forces, and that a cost-based strategy offers less flexibility than a strategy based on differentiation from key competitors.

I am also indebted to my colleagues Paul Beamish, Michael Geringer and Peter Killing for being able to share in their ongoing research into global alliances. Peter Killing's article, "How to Make a Global Joint Venture Work" (*Harvard Business Review*, May-June 1982), and his subsequent working paper, "The Design and Management of International Joint Ventures" (University of Western Ontario, 1989), were especially helpful in writing the final sections of chapter 5.

Finally, an article by Barnaby J. Feder in the *New York Times* (October 8, 1989), entitled "Unfinished Business with Canada," said what is on the minds of many trade negotiators in Canada and the United States. That is, while a lot of companies are rushing to adapt to the realities of free trade, many issues remain unresolved; including the work of harmonization committees, the matter of export subsidies and reaction to the initial judgments of the binational panel. This was a useful introduction to my final chapter.

INDEX

ABOUT THE AUTHOR

HAROLD CROOKELL is Professor of International Business at the University of Western Ontario in London, Ontario. His numerous articles on international business and business-government relations have been published in journals such as *Sloan Management Review*, *Business Quarterly*, and *Canadian Journal of Administrative Science*.